SOUTHERN AFRICA:

The Secret Diplomacy of Detente
South Africa at the Crossroads

COLIN LEGUM

AFRICANA PUBLISHING COMPANY
A division of Holmes & Meier Publishers, Inc
New York

AFRICANA PUBLISHING COMPANY

A Division of Holmes & Meier Publishers Inc.
New York

Published in the United States of America 1975
by Africana Publishing Co
A Division of Holmes & Meier Publishers, Inc
101 Fifth Avenue
New York, New York 10003

Library of Congress Cataloging in Publication Data

Legum, Colin.
  Southern Africa: the secret diplomacy of detente.
  1. Africa, South—Politics and government—1948–   2. Africa,
South—Race question. 3. Africa, South—Foreign relations—Africa, Sub-
Saharan. 4. Africa, Sub-Saharan—Foreign relations—Africa, South. I.
Title.
DT779.9.L43   320.9'68'06   75-22429
                    ISBN 0-8419-0228-3

Printed in Great Britain

Author's Note

This study consists of two chapters which appear in the current volume of the *Africa Contemporary Record* (1974-5). The first is an essay which attempts to reconstruct the history of the secret diplomacy that produced the historic Lusaka Declaration of December 1974. It is obviously still much too early to provide anything like a definitive account of all that went on in the negotiations between President Kenneth Kaunda (Zambia), President Julius Nyerere (Tanzania), President Seretse Khama (Botswana), President Samora Machel (Mozambique) and the Prime Minister of South Africa, Mr Vorster; nevertheless it might be considered useful as an interim exploration of a vitally important chapter in contemporary African history.

The second part consists of an analysis of economic, political and social developments in the Republic of South Africa during the period covered by the previous essay. It provides a background to the diplomacy in which Mr Vorster is now engaged. Anybody wishing to expand their knowledge about current developments in southern Africa should consult the chapters on Zambia, Mozambique, Angola and Tanzania in the 1974 volume of the *Africa Contemporary Record*.

Two major developments have occurred in the discussions over detente since the essay on the secret diplomacy was written in January 1975—the publication of the full record of what transpired during the secret visit by Mr Vorster to Liberia's President Tolbert in *The Times* (London), on 17 February 1975; and the special meeting of the OAU Council of Ministers in Dar es Salaam in April 1975. The outcome of the OAU meeting was a policy document on an *African Strategy in Southern Africa*, based substantially on ideas put forward by the Tanzanian Government. The crux of the strategy is reproduced here:

'African objectives in southern Africa are unchanged. They are: independence for the whole country on the basis of majority rule in both Rhodesia and Namibia; and an end to apartheid and racial discrimination in South Africa.

'Africa's strategy should be to separate the two issues as far as practical, and to give priority to ending the colonial situation in Rhodesia and Namibia.

'In both colonial issues Africa needs to be willing to talk with the South African authorities, and with the local subsidiary authorities, about the mechanics of a transfer of power as soon as there is any evidence of a willingness to accept our objectives in principle. The task of free Africa in this matter is to facilitate the work of the nationalist movement of each country, to provide contact, act as messengers if required, but never to make any commitment on behalf of the nationalists except at their request and never in any way to usurp their authority in their own country.

'But Africa must act as one on this. If necessary we can designate a neighbouring leader and authorize him to act for Africa in relation to both Rhodesia and Namibia, while asking him to keep the rest of Africa in contact with developments as far as possible.

'But whatever progress may or may not be made at any one time in talks about the transfer of power in Rhodesia and Namibia, Africa must be preparing itself for an armed struggle if this becomes necessary, and must be clearly seen to be committed to the armed struggle if the peaceful transfer of power is rejected. Thus Africa needs to be prepared to talk and to negotiate with patience and persistence and skill. But it must also be prepared to support an armed struggle whenever the local nationalist leaders. can show that peaceful methods will not achieve anything. And finally free Africa must do everything possible to help the nationalists of Rhodesia and Namibia achieve and maintain the unity of all nationalist forces. It is not part of free Africa's duty to train and arm the contenders in a future civil war, nor to support one nationalist group in fighting against another.

'Apart from this one case of exploring the chances of peaceful progress to independence on the basis of majority rule in the remaining colonies of southern Africa, free Africa must maintain and strengthen its total boycott of South Africa. Talking with the South African Government on apartheid is worse than irrelevant. We know what Vorster means by it; we know what it means to the African people of South Africa as well as to the whole concept of human equality and dignity. Vorster knows what Africa thinks of apartheid. There is no need for any discussion. Further, if and when a South African Government decides to change its policies and wants to discuss the new direction with the African people, it has no need to use free Africa. Nelson Mandela, Robert Sobukwe and hundreds of other non-white South African leaders are either rotting away physically on Robben Island or in other prisons and places of restriction. When Vorster decides to release these men and women, to allow peaceful African political activity, and to listen to what they say, we shall know that justice might well triumph in South Africa without the bloodshed we fear. Until those signs are evident we must treat South Africa as an outlaw.

'The boycott against South Africa and South African goods will not bring justice to South Africa. It will do no more than show both whites and blacks in South Africa that the free States of this continent refuse to compromise with a denial of human dignity. It will give heart to the non-white peoples to know that their brothers and sisters elsewhere in Africa are conscious of their problem and want to help. Its extension through the world may force the whites to realize that their behaviour leads to isolation from decent human society.

'Let us, the free States of Africa, be united in support of our fellow men who are suffering under colonialism and racialism in South Africa.'

COLIN LEGUM
London, July 1975

PART ONE

THE SECRET DIPLOMACY OF DETENTE IN SOUTHERN AFRICA

Southern Africa: The Secret Diplomacy
Of Detente

COLIN LEGUM

The collapse of Portugal's fascist State on 25 April 1974[1] crucially affected the balance of power in southern Africa and introduced a new element of uncertainty but also of fluidity into a situation of stubborn rigidity. It was a situation that both sides—Black Africa committed to its 'unfinished African revolution', and the two allies, South Africa and Rhodesia, committed to maintaining systems of white political domination—sought to exploit to their own advantage and, at the same time, to reduce the threat of a greater violent confrontation between them.

The elimination of the Portuguese leg of the tripod on which the defenders of the *status quo* in southern Africa had rested their power had a number of significant consequences. First, the black challengers of white power—with their greatly raised morale—could look forward to occupying a strategic area reaching all the way down to the frontiers of South Africa and Namibia, thereby depriving South Africa of the *cordon sanitaire* on which it had relied to keep its own borders insulated against the pressures from the north. (Before the Portuguese collapse South African official spokesmen constantly referred to the *cordon sanitaire* as one of the factors in South Africa's defence favour; now, with its disappearance they suggested that it had never been considered of any real value.)[2] Second, and more immediately crucial, another 300 miles of Rhodesia's frontiers became exposed to pressures from the east as well as the north; instead of the Smith regime being able to rely on Portuguese military assistance to secure their eastern frontier, it was now their black challengers who could expect Portugal's successors—Frelimo—to assist them in their struggle, both through military support and through denying white Rhodesia's imports and exports easy access to the sea. So, white Rhodesia lost doubly: the loss of one of its only two close allies, and the accretion to the strength of their adversaries.

Third, the transfer of power in Angola would similarly expose Namibia's northern frontier at the point where South Africa's control was weakest—in Ovamboland. Fourth, the collapse of Portugal's centuries of colonialism was brought about by armed struggle. Even though it is possible to argue that Portugal's army was not defeated (certainly not in Angola) it is unarguable that the military coup in Lisbon would not have occurred when it did had it not been for Portugal's increasing frustrations, the economic costs and the loss of confidence in the *Novo Estado* caused by the long attrition of the colonial wars. The fact that, when power passed from their hands, Portugal had little alternative but to negotiate with the leaders of the armed struggle in Mozambique, Angola and Guinea-Bissau was of major importance. Finally, the weakened white front brought quick reappraisals in Western capitals about their future policies in the area. South Africa had to reckon on a deteriorating relationship with the West. For example, the arguments of the Washington advisers, whose evaluation of the situation in southern Africa had produced the premise on which the Third Option offered to Dr Kissinger in the controversial National Security Council review of 1970[3], were shot clean out of the water by the developments of early 1974. Their premise had been based on the evaluation that '*the situation in the region is not likely to change appreciably in the foreseeable future,*

2

and in any event we cannot influence it' (p. 32). Nor did the evaluation made by the group of advisers who had argued the premises on which Option Two was based—the one accepted by Kissinger—look very well on the morrow of the Lisbon coup: *'The blacks cannot gain political rights through violence. Constructive change can come only by acquiescence of the white.'* (p. V.)

Both these statements are typical of the evaluation of likely developments in southern Africa which had been made not only in Washington but in most other Western capitals as well. Now, in the Spring of 1974, the North American and European advisers were back at their drawing-boards revising their assessment of the situation—and so were the white Rhodesians and the South Africans.

These changes confronted the regimes in Rhodesia and South Africa with new dangers and more limited options, while offering fresh opportunities for their black challengers. The choice for both sides was clear: either to see their confrontation escalating into greater violence, or to convert it into peaceful negotiations. Both took the second alternative as their first choice, and so produced a climate suitable for detente. The readiness of both sides to establish this priority requires elucidation.

Rhodesia was obviously the most vulnerable target for the next phase of the 'unfinished African revolution'. It was exposed to both military and economic pressures. Eighty per cent of its exports (mainly chrome, tobacco, sugar and coal) pass through Mozambique, with the line to Beira taking c. 1.5 m tons of goods and that to Lourenco Marques taking 2.5 m tons. These exports are vital to Rhodesia's economic survival against the international challenge of sanctions. Of an estimated £100 m worth of Rhodesian exports, about two-thirds went through Mozambique and the rest through South Africa. A Frelimo Government, unlike its predecessoi, would be bound to shut the Rhodesian loophole through Mozambique, and this would throw the entire burden on South Africa. This traffic would be carried over the hurriedly completed new light-guage Rutenga-Beit Bridge link and the Mafeking line through Botswana. But Sir Seretse Khama's Government had been quick to show its unwillingness for this to happen by proposing to take over the vital stretch of the line traversing Botswana. South Africa's already over-congested ports could not easily handle the additional traffic from Rhodesia. Smith got his first intimation of a new South Africa stand when he went to talk with Vorster in August about the problems now facing the two countries. Vorster told Smith that he could offer him no preference for his exports passing through the South African communications' system. Later in August, Smith sent three Ministers for talks to Cape Town, on railway questions; but they met with no more success.

Rhodesia's 1974-5 Budget deficit was just under £33 m (R52.9 m). This had to be met in part by a heavy 10% retrospective war financing surcharge on 1973-4 personal and corporate tax, which would reduce it only by just over one-third. Its security force had gone up to 58,000; and the country was spending 15.6% of its total Budget on defence—c. £64 m (R100.5 m). It has had to pay out a minimum of £14 m (R23.4 m) annually in subsidies and compensation for loss of sales of commodities hit by sanctions—excluding the heavy subsidy for the railways; all this it managed to do only by sharply increasing the level of its public debt.

Clearly, therefore, the prospect of an intensified guerrilla struggle, into which the OAU would put all the financial and military resources which had previously gone to the anti-Portuguese forces (plus the active support in weapons, military bases and guerrilla officers which Frelimo could offer) coinciding with a crunching intensification of economic sanctions, would severely reduce the Smith regime's chances of survival—unless its South African ally agreed to commit itself to a massive economic and military rescue operation. But South Africa's own options had also been reduced.

3

South Africa needs to establish good relations with its new Frelimo-dominated neighbour for three reasons: the value of Lourenco Marques in relieving South Africa's over-congested ports; the need for a continued flow of migrant workers from Mozambique who account for 25% of its total mine labour force; and the need for the important supply of energy from Cabora Bassa, about to come on flow. It also needs to try and persuade Frelimo not to allow Mozambique to be used as a base for guerrilla attacks across South Africa's frontiers into Zululand and the eastern Transvaal. Through early diplomatic contacts Frelimo had made the withdrawal of South Africa's 2,000 para-military police from Rhodesia a prerequisite for any future negotiations.

On its frontier with Angola, South Africa also needs good relations with whatever government finally emerges there. Its security position in Namibia especially in Ovamboland—would be seriously threatened by a hostile Angola's support for Swapo's guerrilla forces. Moreover, South Africa was increasingly compelled to consider the international implications of a major military struggle in Namibia. It is already in serious straits at the UN where even its last Western friends, even France, now all support the Security Council's decision declaring South Africa's rule of Namibia to be illegal.

While inside the Republic the economy was further strengthened by the rise in the price of gold and the Government's hold on its white electorate was unassailable, it was confronted by a new-found militancy among black urban workers, a challenging attitude among the Bantustan leaders and by the rise of Black Consciousness among African youth—all pointers to a growing confrontation inside the Republic which reflected—though of course not yet matching—the confrontation outside its borders.

The most pressing fear, however, was over Rhodesia. If the Smith regime would not—or could not allow itself to—see the shape of the coming struggle clearly, the Vorster regime could afford to be much more realistic about it. Their assessment was that white minority rule in Rhodesia was doomed; any attempt by South Africa to rescue it would involve the Republic in an open-ended military and economic commitment, and with no guarantee of success. What was much more likely was that South Africa and Rhodesia would find themselves in a white-black military confrontation; South Africa's Western friends would become even more critical, or even hostile; and black Africa's friends and would-be political backers (including the Arabs and the communist countries) would be likely to become more closely involved in the area. Thus Frelimo's pre-condition for any future talks with South Africa—the withdrawal of South Africa's military police presence from Rhodesia—had also become a South African national interest.

However, if Vorster were to withdraw his semi-military force, he would have to be able to do so 'honourably', i.e. in a way that would not upset his own white electorate and, possibly, trigger off a white backlash against him at home, which would undoubtedly be fed by angry white Rhodesian cries of 'betrayal'. The only 'honourable' way out of the Rhodesian trap was through a negotiated settlement of the nine-year old constitutional crisis. The logic of this evaluation was that South Africa's interests might coincide with at least some of the interests of its black neighbours, especially Zambia, Botswana, Malawi and Mozambique. But it would at the same time produce a sharp conflict of interest between Pretoria and Salisbury—unless, somehow, Mr Smith could be made to see Rhodesia's future as realistically as did his last ally. Thus the old tripartite White Alliance was about to disappear, with South Africa now concerned about buying enough time to pursue its own national interests while heading off a military confrontation with Black Africa.

On the African side a similar reappraisal of future possibilities was proceeding independently. Frelimo—which had assumed responsibility for a transitional

4

government pending Mozambique's full independence in June 1975—found that it had inherited a bankrupt country; and even more worrying, it was about to inherit a colonial-type economy which had left the country's subsistence agriculture sector largely undeveloped.[4] It would require years to build an effective rural-based economy. Meanwhile, it was faced with a number of urgent economic and political decisions. Clearly, it had no option but to block Rhodesia's exports; this would bring virtual ruin to Beira, 80% of whose traffic depended on Rhodesia. If it were also to cut off South Africa's trade, this would mean that its second port, Lourenco Marques, would also be crippled since c. 75% of its traffic comes from South Africa. If both ports were to be substantially run down it would mean massive unemployment, loss of revenue and less efficient harbour services for Mozambique itself.

Frelimo's other dilemma was over the future of its migrant workers to the South African mines since their remitted earnings constitute the largest single source of foreign earnings; to cut this off at a time of acute economic need could spell short-term disaster, or the need to ask for considerable foreign aid. Less acute, but none the less important, was what to do about the colonial-conceived Cabora Bassa hydro-electric project nearing completion. Frelimo had from the start declared its total opposition to this project and had done its best to halt its construction. Having failed in this aim, they had become the inheritors of what, for an independent Mozambique, was something of a white elephant. Its huge energy output greatly exceeded the country's foreseeable needs; but its potentialities for irrigation could be usefully exploited. South Africa—which had largely inspired the project and had invested heavily in its construction—badly needed its energy output. For Frelimo this dilemma was a painful one: if it agreed to sell the energy to South Africa it would be contributing to some extent to helping the Republic's further economic growth; not to do so would leave Mozambique with an expensive inheritance that could not be fully utilized. For all these reasons, Frelimo found that it had certain mutual interests with South Africa in establishing, at least, a viable trading relationship.

Malawi was caught in the middle.[5] Having initially chosen to maintain friendly relations with Portuguese Mozambique—for Dr Banda's own particularist interests—its relations with Frelimo were not of the best, nor were they good with its other African neighbours. The change in southern Africa required that Dr Banda should try and establish better relations with his neighbours while still retaining his 'special relationship' with South Africa.

Zambia and Tanzania—Frelimo's most committed backers—were in complete sympathy with its need to remain on as good terms as possible with South Africa, at least during the difficult transition period after independence. They could see no value in an independent but economically broken-backed and, hence, politically unstable Mozambique. Judged from southern Africa's long-term interests it was better to ensure a potentially stable Mozambique even if it involved making some compromises with South Africa than to see its independence stunted from the beginning.

Zambia, which had made considerable economic sacrifices in opposing the Rhodesian rebellion, had a strong interest in helping to promote a political settlement in the area. Its first priority was to achieve a settlement of the Rhodesian problem. Furthermore, President Kaunda and President Nyerere have all along expressed their preference for a peaceful settlement of the racial conflicts of southern Africa over that of an increasingly violent conflict. This preference had been spelled out in the Lusaka Manifesto of 1967,[6] which was subsequently adopted as official OAU policy. It offered Portugal, Rhodesia and South Africa a chance for peaceful negotiations as an alternative to a violent resolution of their differences, but that offer had been rejected by all three. Once the new regime in Lisbon indicated its readiness to abandon Portugal's colonial role, the African States had unanimously showed their willingness to co-operate in achieving a peaceful transition to independence of all the Portuguese colonies in Africa. Having demonstrated their goodwill in this way they felt the time was once again opportune to explore the peaceful alternatives set out in the Lusaka Manifesto. This time their offer would find a readier response, at least in Pretoria, for the reasons described earlier.

So, step by step, the stage was set for the opening of a new chapter of detente. It is still too early to describe in all its details or with complete accuracy all the steps taken in the secret diplomacy to achieve detente; what follows, therefore, should be taken as an initial contribution to, rather than a definitive account of, the period's secret diplomacy.

Vorster's reaction to Portugal's capitulation of its colonial role was coolly statesmanlike. He at once held out a hand of friendship to a new Frelimo Government. 'A black Government in Mozambique holds no fears for us whatever' was to become the theme of his new policy; and he proved his *bona fides* by refusing to encourage an abortive white-led counter-revolution in Mozambique, or by taking any steps which might add to the country's transitional difficulties. Asked how he viewed the disorder and economic chaos which had threatened Mozambique and Angola in the months after Portugal's change of policy, he replied: 'I don't like it. Unrest in any part of the world gives cause for concern, especially in a neighbouring country. Whoever takes over in Mozambique has a tough task ahead of him. It will require exceptional leadership. They have my sympathy and I wish them well.'[7]

Meanwhile, Vorster lost no time in trying to resume the dialogue with African leaders which had started in 1970—with an African initiative coming mainly from Dr Banda and the President of the Ivory Coast, Felix Houphouet-Boigny. That mistimed initiative—and, in the view of a majority of African leaders, a misconceived one—had been killed by the OAU.[8] Sometime in the middle of 1974 South Africa's Foreign Minister, Dr Hilgard Muller, undertook a number of secret diplomatic moves with the Ivorians; he was assisted by the French, whose close growing economic and military involvement in South Africa[9] gave them a special interest in promoting a detente through their African Francophone contacts. Muller later disclosed in a statement to the South Africa Parliament (12 September 1974) that he had held meetings in July with African leaders 'in States not bordering on South Africa'. He also said that he had held meetings with 'two advisers of a distant African State', but without disclosing their identity. Dr Muller paid a special tribute to Houphouet-Boigny, whose farsightedness, he said, had paved the way for dialogue and detente. His contacts resulted in Vorster embarking at the end of September on a secret mission with a staff of fifteen members for five days of talks in a number of African countries. The secret was so well kept that nothing at all about it leaked out until December, and even now the actual itinerary is still not known. But it seems likely that the South African party visited the Ivory Coast, possibly Gabon, Botswana and Salisbury. Separate contacts were also made with President Banda in Malawi. In the Ivory Coast, talks were held with Houphouet-Boigny and President Senghor of Senegal. Although Houphouet has denied these talks, Senghor confirmed that he had contacts with Mr Vorster and liberal South African aides, 'for progress can only be made by discussion, and any solution requires negotiation between both parties . . . The fundamental problem is a nationality one. But I do not despair of seeing a solution'.[10]

By late September Vorster had begun to persuade Smith that the time had come to change tack. Meanwhile, an independent initiative was undertaken by President Kaunda working in close tandem with President Nyerere, Sir Seretse Khama,

President Mobutu of Zaire and Frelimo's leader, Samora Machel.[11] Nyerere and Kaunda met for strategy sessions (with Samora Machel present at some of the meetings) in May, June and July, to assess the new realities of Rhodesia's position in particular.

In this phase the black Rhodesian leaders were not consulted (partly for security reasons). But in October the exile leaders of Frolizi, Zapu and Zanu in Lusaka were contacted. According to a Frolizi source they were told simply of the contacts and that it was felt there was some possibility of making advances on the Rhodesian issue and thereby averting a full-scale guerrilla war. It was stressed that nothing positive had occurred, but that South Africa was being used as the Trojan Horse. Asked if they approved of the initiative, they gave their agreement in general terms. From what transpired it is clear that by this point Botswana's President, Sir Seretse Khama, was also involved.

On 10 August Zambia's Foreign Minister, Vernon Mwaanga, began to involve Britain in the new African initiative. He travelled especially to Geneva to see the British Foreign and Commonwealth Secretary, Mr James Callaghan, who was at that time engaged in negotiations for a settlement of the Cyprus crisis. Mwaanga proposed that a group of four—Zambia, Tanzania, Botswana and Britain—should be established at official level to review the Rhodesian situation and see if there was any room for progress. The African leaders would guarantee the security and property of the white Rhodesian minority and would accept a transitional period leading to majority rule and independence for Rhodesia provided a settlement could be negotiated which provided for this ultimate objective. Callaghan warmly welcomed this initiative and Mwaanga went on to Washington where he was one of the few black Foreign Ministers to meet privately with Kissinger. Meanwhile exploratory talks were going on with Vorster through intermediaries. Among these was Mr Harry Oppenheimer and his Anglo-American representative in Lusaka, Dr Zac de Beer. A crucial figure in the South African team of intermediaries was Gen. Hendrik van den Bergh, the head of BOSS, the Bureau for State Security, who was especially concerned about the intelligence side of the negotiations. But Kaunda—remembering Vorster's betrayal of confidence when he disclosed to Parliament his secret exchanges with Zambia following an earlier attempt to promote a settlement in 1971[12]—moved cautiously. It was not until early November that Kaunda risked sending his personal envoy, Mark Chona, to Cape Town for the first of several contacts with Vorster. Either on this visit or on a second visit later in November he presented Vorster with eight proposals representing the 'demands' of the Rhodesian nationalists. These demands, which were later to become a source of controversy, were disclosed by the ANC on 12 January 1975. They were:

1-4. Release of all political detainees, restrictees, other political prisoners, exiles, and those under sentence of death for essentially political crimes.
5. Lifting of the ban on Zapu, Zanu and all black nationalist organizations.
6. All political trials to be halted.
7. Creation of conditions for free political activity.
8. Lifting of the state of emergency.

Meanwhile, October had been a critical month. While the secret talks to establish a new kind of relationship between South Africa and black Africa were producing some evidence of willingness from both sides to move towards detente, the OAU was engaged at the UN General Assembly in trying to get South Africa expelled from the world body. This move failed in the end only because of the triple veto cast by the US, UK and France. But the episode also made a positive contribution for two reasons:

7

first, South Africa was seriously worried about the possibility of expulsion and virtual diplomatic isolation; and second, the US and UK had both exploited the opportunity provided by the use of their veto in saving South Africa from expulsion to press on the Republic the need for fundamental change and joined in the unanimous Security Council Resolution of 15 December that gave South Africa until 1 May to take a series of actions to encourage Namibian self-determination. The US Assistant Secretary of State, Donald Easum, was travelling in southern Africa in late October and early November. While his public statements were largely concerned with explaining the reasons for the veto on the move to expel South Africa from the UN, his statements were to assure both black Africa and South Africa of his support for the moves towards detente.

Earlier, on 10 June 1974, Vorster had first indicated a different approach to the UN over Namibia. Speaking in his own constituency in Nigel he had said: 'This Government and Governments before it have never shied away from the fact that South West Africa possessed an international character.' While this affirmation was not in itself new, it was given a different meaning by his undertaking that: *'It is not the Government of South Africa's task or function to decide the future of SWA, but South Africa will also not permit any outsider to do so.'*[13] The decision, he added, would be left to 'every individual and to the peoples' in the territory.

By then it had become clear that Vorster had abandoned his earlier proposal to promote a series of mini-States in Namibia: the new aim was to divide the territory into two independent States—Ovamboland in the north and a federal republic of Namibia's white and black 'provinces' in the rest of the country. Clearly, however, this was a tactical ploy rather than a plan that could possibly hope to carry the support either of 'the peoples' or of the UN. The possibility of a complete South African withdrawal, under certain circumstances, had begun to take shape.[14]

Vorster's most significant speech to date was the one he delivered to his Senate on 23 October 1974.[15] He had especially invited the entire diplomatic corps in Cape Town to be present for the occasion. 'Southern Africa,' he said, 'is at the crossroads and should choose now between peace and escalating violence'. The cost of confrontation would be 'high—too high for southern Africa to pay'. On Rhodesia he said: 'It is in the interests of all the parties to find a solution.' And on Namibia: 'South Africa would not withdraw suddenly.' He still believed that 'the only solution to the territory's problems was that the people must be allowed to decide for themselves'. He elaborated on the basic strategy of South Africa's policy: the creation of 'a United Nations of Southern African States' which would include the independent 'black nations' of South Africa (the Bantustans), Namibia, Rhodesia and the former High Commission territories and, hopefully, Mozambique, Angola and Zambia. The dream of a South African Economic Community had become, for Vorster, a potential reality if detente prospered. This has become a crucial determinant of South Africa's policy—a policy which, needless to say, is not shared by the Africans engaged in the moves towards detente: their aim is to secure the independence of an undivided, multi-racial State in South Africa—as in Rhodesia and Namibia.

Despite these conflicting interests between the two sides, they had come to share a mutual interest in meanwhile reducing the possibilities of a violent confrontation. The price demanded for this on the African side was stated by Zambia's Foreign Minister, Vernon Mwaanga:[16] 'The minimum—I call them fundamental—changes which could open the way to peace are South Africa's complete disengagement in Rhodesia—and termination of her illegal occupation of Namibia. She must hand Namibia over to the United Nations.'

On the day following Vorster's speech to his Senate, 24 October, South Africa's

8

Representative at the UN, Pik Botha, replying to the General Assembly debate on the proposal to expel South Africa, adopted a fresh approach: 'Let us not delude ourselves—there are no easy solutions. But my Government stands ready to explore all avenues which may bring about an understanding among us . . . Nor is our policy inflexible—it postulates a certain broad direction, the end of which is sovereign independence for the peoples concerned. There is no question of forcing together peoples who do not wish to be joined. Equally, there is no question of keeping apart peoples who wish to come together. The real point at issue is therefore not one of objective, but of method: the best practical way of ensuring self-determination and human development.'

After admitting that 'unsavoury and reprehensible incidents between blacks and whites do occur in South Africa, incidents which no civilized man can defend', and adding that 'for every unsavoury incident which may occur, there are many more which negate the accusation that the whites of South Africa have a callous disregard for the dignity and feeling of blacks', he went on to make the statement which was subsequently latched onto as representing a crucial change of policy on South Africa's part: 'Mr President, we *do* have discriminatory practices and we *do* have discriminatory laws. And it is precisely because of this that the greatest misunderstandings occur and our motives are most misrepresented. But that discrimination, must not be equated with racialism. If we *have* that discrimination, it is not because the whites in South Africa have any *herrenvolk* complex. We are not better than the black people, we are not cleverer than they are. What we can achieve, so can they. Those laws and practices are a part of the historical evolution of our country—they were introduced to avoid friction and to promote and protect the interests and the development of every group—not only those of the whites. But I want to state here today very clearly and categorically: My Government does *not* condone discrimination purely on the grounds of race or colour. Discrimination based solely on the colour of a man's skin cannot be defended. *And we shall do everything in our power to move away from discrimination based on race or colour* . . . Mr President, I would mislead you if I were to imply that this will happen overnight. There are schools of thought, traditions and practices which cannot be changed overnight. But we are moving in that direction. We shall continue to do so.'

It was this section in Botha's speech, following closely on Vorster's statement of the day before, that led President Kaunda on 26 October to welcome '*the voice of reason for which Africa and the rest of the world has been waiting*'. To persuade Vorster to move further he offered Zambia's help to remove obstacles to peace in the area. Kaunda's response was eagerly followed up by Vorster and his Foreign Minister who said: 'It is possible that we are on the threshold of a new era of peace, co-operation and development in southern Africa.'

Now the way was opened for more intensive exchanges between Lusaka and Cape Town in an effort to reduce the rhetoric about the need for detente to a practical formula for the settlement of the Rhodesian problem as a first step.

These exchanges were so hopeful that Mr Vorster boldly proclaimed, in replying to his critics, at another speech he made in Nigel on 10 November: '*I wonder if they will listen if I say give South Africa a six months' chance by not making our road harder than it is already. I say, if you give South Africa a chance, you will be surprised where we will stand.*' This remarkable statement came as much of a surprise to Vorster's own supporters as it did to his African partners in the search for detente since they understood him to be forecasting radical changes *inside* South Africa itself. In fact, as was only too soon to become clear, he was referring only to South Africa's relations to other States in southern Africa. This was confirmed by his Minister of Information and Interior, Dr Connie Mulder who said, in a speech on 12

November, that Vorster's speech had caused 'panic in some circles' (It had been criticized by prominent Old Guard members of the ruling party). There was, Dr Mulder assured the nation at large, no need for 'panic' since the Prime Minister's 'six months' speech had 'referred to developments in Africa and in the field of foreign relations, and was in no way intended to lead to the disappearance of Separate Development.[17]

Vorster himself put the record straight on 16 November when he said 'in a spirit of great friendliness to black leaders' that: 'If there are people who are telling you that the Government is planning to allow a one-man-one-vote system in South Africa and, by so doing, create a multi-racial Parliament, they are misleading you. *That will never happen*.' And for good measure he added that 'it was a cardinal principle of Nationalist policy that no group dared to allow political power to slip out of its hands.'[18] Apartheid, in the shape of Separate Development, was there to stay.

But whatever troubles Vorster's policies were running him into at home they did not affect his moves towards detente: the goal was still set for a settlement in Rhodesia. Vorster was at the centre of two lines of communications—one to Smith, the other to Kaunda. During Mark Chona's second visit to Cape Town in November, Vorster apparently told him that the black Rhodesians' eight demands (see above), did not pose any great difficulty and that he would persuade Smith to accept them. Smith's only condition in this phase appears to have been that a cease-fire was a prerequisite to everything. Unfortunately his definition of what this entailed, and what the Rhodesian nationalists understood by it were at variance. Chona returned to Lusaka and it was at this point, in the earlier part of November, that Kaunda asked for the imprisoned Rhodesian leaders to be brought to Lusaka. Vorster arranged this and Mark Chona, accompanied by President Julius Nyere's private secretary, Joseph Butiku, flew in a special plane to Salisbury to collect them. He saw Smith who is believed to have told Chona that 'unity was impossible among the nationalists'; wagging his finger under the Zambian's nose, he said: 'If you can achieve unity you can come back and cut this finger off.' Some Zambians believe that the reason Smith allowed them to go to Lusaka at all was because he was certain unity was impossible, and that their joint agreement appears to have been the second of Smith's preconditions for talks.

Chona received a rude shock when he went to Salisbury prison to collect Sithole and Nkomo, who had been transferred there. Sithole would not speak. (He had also failed to answer Nkomo's questions at a prison meeting two days earlier). Two other detainees Robert Mugabe, Zanu's secretary-general, and Morton Malianga were also brought to see Chona. They broke the news to him that Sithole was no longer the leader of Zanu. Chona had no choice but to fly back to Lusaka with Bishop Muzorewa, Nkomo, and with Robert Mugabe representing Zanu. But Nyerere, Kaunda, Khama and Machel refused to deal with the Zanu executive members; they were rusticated to a room in State House. Muzorewa and Nkomo were briefed on developments and returned to Salisbury.

On 13 November Sithole was flown to Lusaka. The Zanu delegation had not explained why Sithole was no longer Zanu leader, but they told other nationalists in December that Sithole had suffered considerably in detention and had proposed to renounce all political activity in return for his freedom. As a result he had been removed as Zanu leader by his colleagues in prison three weeks before Chona went to collect him. This was obviously highly embarrassing for the independent Africans trying to forge a united front. Zanu's executive members were prevailed upon to withdraw the suspension.

An astonished world therefore discovered—when the well-kept secret leaked out some weeks later—that Smith had released six of his political prisoners to be flown to

Lusaka in a South African aircraft for their talks with the African Presidents. The ice was broken. Smith, who had for so long described Nkomo and Sithole as the kind of people with whom he would never sit down around the same table, was now allowing them to play a central role in discussing the country's future. At the same time he denied that any South African pressure was being exerted on him. Both his regime and South Africa agreed that a settlement would be desirable 'in order to bring about as much normality as possible in southern Africa. There is no difference of opinion between us'.[19]

At the beginning of December the Rhodesian nationalists returned again to Lusaka; this time there was also a white Rhodesian delegation led by Jack Gaylard, and a South African delegation led by the head of its Foreign Ministry, Brand Fourie. They had separate talks with the Presidents. After some tough bargaining on Friday, 6 December, an agreement was reached whereby Frolizi, Zanu and Zapu would be dissolved and reformed under the ANC umbrella. It was suggested that Nkomo should become president, Muzorewa vice-president, and Sithole secretary-general.

Agreement was also reached—or was thought to have been reached—over the immediate steps to be taken to settle the Rhodesian problem. This provided, in essence, for cessation of all guerrilla activities, release of all African political prisoners once violence had stopped (there was some confusion over the timing of this), summoning of a constitutional conference without any preconditions, and South Africa's withdrawal of its 'police' forces once all violence had ended.

Smith was due to address the nation on Sunday, 8 December, and Nkomo was to make an announcement in Salisbury on 9 December which would stress majority rule and racial harmony. But when the Rhodesian nationalist leaders re-assembled on Friday night, 6 December, Sithole announced that his executive would not agree to Zanu's dissolution. They argued until late in the evening, and Sithole was finally sent back to convince his executive. While Frolizi, as the smallest party, stood only to gain by unity, (and with Nkomo committed to it and to Zapu) Zanu stood to lose most. For two years they had organized the guerrilla war but they would not be quite so dominant when it came to constitutional talks. To complicate the situation further there was a power struggle within Zanu's leadership in which its exile leader, Herbert Chitepo, was the critical figure. Apparently (probably in October) he had seen Nyerere and suggested that the Rhodesian detainees should not be freed immediately as he feared they would only cause disunity. Nyerere's reaction was such that he refused even to speak to Chitepo on the early December flight to Lusaka from Dar es Salaam. During this flight Chipeto gave his 'we will not negotiate' interview to James Macmanus of *The Guardian*, who happened to be on the same plane. While Chitepo later denied that he had said this, one of the Tanzanian delegation had overheard the conversation on the plane.

On Saturday, 7 December, the Rhodesian nationalists had been called into plenary session by the three Presidents. Sithole informed them that Zanu would still not agree, and Nyerere lost his temper—which can be fearsome. He particularly attacked Chitepo, demanding 'who is this modern Napoleon?' He accused Zanu of being 'married to disunity', and apparently accused Chitepo of wanting civil war in Rhodesia 'to kill his brother Africans so that he could emerge as a leader'. He castigated him for suggesting that his brother Africans should be left to rot in detention and warned Zanu they would get no support from the three Presidents. Nyerere's salutary castigation lasted for two hours, and when he stopped Kaunda started on a similar theme. Nyerere and Seretse Khama flew home after lunch, and Kaunda went back to his lodge, leaving the black Rhodesians stunned by the ferocity of the attack. They, in their turn, began to castigate each other before accepting the

ANC secretary-general, Dr Chavanduka, as chairman. Within three hours a unity agreement was reached and they phoned Mark Chona. Kaunda would not at first believe the good news; but later when he saw the nationalists at his lodge and saw the agreement, he immediately threw a banquet. He phoned Nyerere the next morning to tell him about the agreement which was to be signed on the following Tuesday; Nyerere apparently told him to get it signed immediately before anyone again changed his mind!

These disputes within the black Rhodesian front did not, however, directly affect the agreement that had been reached between the African Presidents, the Rhodesian nationalists, Smith's and Vorster's representatives. All was still set for the agreement to be announced on 18 December. Instead, Smith issued a statement saying the negotiations had collapsed; he put the blame for it on Nyerere. His wild allegation is not supported by what had, in fact, happened.

On 5 December three Rhodesian officials flew to Lusaka—Gaylard, Smith and O'Neill—and were taken in to see the three African Presidents at about 4 p.m. in State House. Nyerere was chairman of the meeting and, at the direct request of the black Rhodesians, had put their position on the proposed constitutional talks.

1. That majority rule was not negotiable.
2. That independence was not negotiable.
3. That all that was negotiable was the machinery for the transfer of power to the African majority.

This is what Smith really rejected. Vorster hurriedly intervened and sent an envoy to Lusaka on Monday, 8 December. A compromise was reached that neither side would lay down preconditions for constitutional talks.

And so the Lusaka agreement was finally reached. On 10 December, Smith told Rhodesia he was releasing the black nationalist leaders, having received a guarantee that 'terrorist activity in Rhodesia will cease immediately and the proposed constitutional conference will take place without preconditions'. That is not strictly accurate. Smith had demanded a ceasefire in which the guerrillas would surrender their arms and withdraw from Rhodesia. This was rejected. The four Rhodesian nationalist leaders, in a statement before they flew back, said: 'As a demonstration of our sincerity, all freedom fighters will be instructed, *as soon as a date for negotiations has been fixed*, to suspend fighting.' The ceasefire was really a stand-off, with neither side withdrawing; but they would not seek each other out. A *de facto* ceasefire came into effect from 11 December; but only when the date for talks was agreed would the nationalist leaders move to the second stage of publicly telling the guerrillas to stop fighting for the duration of the talks.

This misinterpretation, or misunderstanding, over the actual terms of the ceasefire was to produce further difficulties in January 1975 when some violence continued and four South African policemen were killed; this naturally enraged Vorster. It also enabled Smith to accuse his opponents of not keeping their side of the agreement.

When the British Foreign Secretary arrived in Lusaka on his African visit early in January 1975, the prospects for detente seemed to be receding. Kaunda and Vorster were in close contact, each side trying to influence their respective allies—but Vorster, because of the loss of his own policemen, was not perhaps leaning as hard on Smith as he might otherwise have done. Kaunda encouraged Callaghan to go to South Africa to try and persuade Smith to honour his part of the agreement, while Kaunda and Nyerere pursued their efforts to get the Zimbabwean guerrillas to disengage. Vorster, though angry, was not unhelpful in his talks with Callaghan: for him the need is still for a Rhodesian settlement as the necessary first step towards detente, the de-escalation of violence, peaceful relations with his neighbours, and the fulfilment of his dream of a Southern African Economic Community. What South

Africa needs, above all else, for its strategy to succeed is time and a non-violent relationship with black Africa.

By early 1975 the chief stumbling-block in the way of Vorster's strategy was Smith—his erstwhile ally. This ruptured friendship is easily explained. So long as the White Alliance had held up in southern Africa, the national interests of Rhodesia and South Africa, as conceived by their present regimes, were mutual. But once detente seemed possible, and with the new changes in southern Africa precipitated by Portugal's withdrawal, their interests began to diverge. It is understandable that Vorster should accept that 'white minority rule' in Rhodesia is expendable if this were felt to be essential to the interests of his own white-dominated political system. But the liquidation of minority rule in Rhodesia—the entrenchment of which, after all, was the *raison d'etre* for the rebellion called out by Smith—was not an acceptable way out for the Rhodesian Front.

Vorster could argue—with considerable justification—that the best interests of both the white communities in South Africa and Rhodesia is to ensure a peaceful transition to majority rule in Rhodesia; and, moreover, that this is the *most* that might be hoped for in the new situation. He could back up his arguments by withholding from Smith the kind of support he needs to delay majority rule for so long as possible. But there were constraints on Vorster pursuing such a policy. His own electorate, and elements within his own ruling party, need to be convinced about the wisdom of 'selling out' the white Rhodesians; they could argue—as some of them did—that today it would be the white Rhodesians, and the day after the white South Africans; and that the black appetite for majority rule would not stop on the northern banks of the Limpopo River. And who can deny that they are right? But Vorster can argue that white Rhodesia is, in any event, doomed—whatever South Africa does—and that his own policies offer the best hope of winning the time needed to achieve his own Government's long-term aims. These were succinctly des-cribed by South Africa's Ambassador in London, Dr Carl de Wet:[20] 'I foresee South Africa with one white government and, say, twelve independent black African nations adjoining her. Hopefully, they will be friendly, bound in some sort of loose economic federation, not unlike the EEC. Who knows, maybe there will be a Treaty of Pretoria. Once we have sorted out all the constitutional problems involved in nationhood then I think the sky's the limit.'

Vorster's reappraisal of policy, and the parting of South Africa's ways with white Rhodesia, put Smith in an impossible position. He needs South Africa's help to survive, but he refuses to pay South Africa's price. With a hostile Government in South Africa he cannot possibly hope to survive. Meanwhile, white Rhodesia might lose its only chance of a slower and peaceful transition to majority rule if the quarrel between Pretoria and Smith should become exacerbated. There seemed, by early 1975, only one way out for Smith: that he should go through the motions of negotiating with the black Rhodesian leaders, while refusing to submit to their demands; and that he should use this period to try and influence a change of policy in the South African Government—either by compelling Vorster to rethink his policies because of the growing pressures from his *verkramptes*, or to cause Vorster to resign in favour of somebody less likely to sacrifice the 'interests' of white Rhodesia for the sake of white South Africa's interests. It is an ironic, if piquant, development.

1. See essay on *Portugal's Year in Africa 1974* in this volume.
2. Cf Dr Connie Mulder, South Africa's Minister of Interior and Information.
3. National Security Council Interdepartmental Group for Africa: Study in Response to National Security Study Memorandum 39: Southern Africa; AF/NSC—1G 69; 15 August 1969. Sent by Dr Kissinger to President Nixon on 1 February 1970.

4. See chapter on Mozambique in this volume.
5. See chapter on Malawi in this volume.
6. See *Africa Contemporary Record (ACR)* 1969–70 p. C 41.
7. *Newsweek*, Washington; 16 September 1974.
8. See ACR 1971–2: *Dialogue: The Great Debate*: p. A 66.
9. See essay on *France's Year in Africa* in this volume.
10. *Le Matin*, 15 December 1974.
11. I am much indebted to my colleague David Martin for information about the diplomacy leading up to, and including, the Lusaka talks.
12. *ACR* 1971–72, pp. 13.
13. *Windhoek Advertiser*, 11 June 1974.
14. See chapter on Namibia in this volume.
15. *Rand Daily Mail*, 24 October 1974.
16. *Rand Daily Mail*, 4 November 1974.
17. *Sunday Times* (Johannesburg), 17 November 1974.
18. *Rand Daily Mail*, 18 November 1974.
19. Ian Smith interview with *Financial Mail* (Johannesburg) 15 November 1974.
20. *The Director*, London; January 1975.

PART TWO

SOUTH AFRICA AT THE CROSSROADS

1974-5

South Africa at the Crossroads 1974-5

Against all the evidence of recent years[1] showing that the Republic was getting into deeper trouble, the image of South Africa as a stable country, largely invulnerable to external forces, persisted until 1974 when these illusions were finally dispelled by a combination of internal explosions and external pressures. At home, pressures were built up by black industrial unrest, the challenge of Homeland leaders, and the defiance of militant black students and Coloured leaders; abroad, the pressures resulting from the collapse of Portuguese colonialism were felt not only in the significant change in the balance of power in southern Africa but also in the Western response to this new situation. All these developments gave greater reality to the chronic fears of white South Africans about their possible isolation both in the continent and in the wider world community. The *cordon sanitaire*—which had served the purpose of a moat around the *laager*'s outer periphery—ceased to exist with the collapse of Pretoria's faithful old Lisbon ally; and the Republic survived a move to expel it from the UN thanks only to a combined veto cast by Britain, the United States and France.

There was a special irony in the timing of this great reversal of the Republic's political fortunes since the greatly increased world price of gold had freed its economy from the perennial anxieties about its foreign exchange earnings: at the moment when its economic future looked most golden, its political future grew darker.

The Lisbon coup on 25 April[2] coincided with the massive electoral victory of the ruling Afrikaner National Party. In terms of political and economic power—as well as of military strength—Afrikanerdom was still on the ascendant; but in terms of its effective power over the black majority at home and in confrontation with black challengers abroad, its actual power had declined. The shock of Portugal conceding victory to the armed guerrilla movements—especially in neighbouring Mozambique—was, however, lessened by the imaginative leadership of the Prime Minister, Mr Vorster, who was remarkably quick to evaluate realistically the dangers of the new situation; he immediately sought ways of winning African support—strictly outside the Republic, not within it—in order to reduce the sharper risks of military confrontation. Only after his efforts had borne some early fruit did he feel sufficiently confident to call on the country to face the fact that: 'Southern Africa is at a crossroads, and should choose now between peace or escalating violence.' The cost of confrontation, he went on to tell his Senate on 3 October 1974, would be 'too high for southern Africa to pay'.

In other words, Vorster's response to the new situation was to seek a detente with Black Africa. The price for a real detente by most African leaders was too high for Vorster to accept since it demanded of him fundamental changes inside SA itself. But the secret diplomacy that went on between April and October 1974 disclosed a possible area for negotiations—Rhodesia and Namibia. This 'breakthrough' gave Vorster the chance he needed to restore white South African morale; to Africans it gave a chance of two fairly quick, non-violent victories which would leave SA completely exposed to the forces of Africans at home and in the rest of the continent. Vorster's detente diplomacy is discussed fully elsewhere in this volume.[3]

White and black South Africa debated what lessons there were for the Republic in what had happened to Portugal. Predictably they reached different conclusions. But

16

the differences were not only between whites and blacks. The Opposition leader, Sir de Villiers Graaff, warned in Parliament in September that the events in Portugal's African territories had drastically reduced 'both the time and the space which stood between SA and the relentless approach of armed insurgency'. The lessons he suggested the Prime Minister should learn were: that 'time was of the essence'; that 'traditional concepts and outmoded policies, however firmly and sincerely held, could create a dangerous mental blockage in adapting swiftly to changing events'; that Portugal's 'stubborn delay in seeking a remedy for the isolation of the growing international hostility which had impeded her revival were undoubted causes of the sudden collapse of her policies'; and that 'the creation of representative institutions in name only and without real responsibilities was dangerous because there was no real sharing of power.' While the Prime Minister agreed there were lessons to be learnt from the Portuguese experience, he suggested they were quite different from those mentioned by the Opposition leader. In his view Portugal's African policies were to a great extent those of the Progressive Party and also of the official Opposition, and 'diametrically opposed' to those of the SA Government. In other words, he felt that the correct lesson was the importance of pursuing the path of apartheid.

There were to be two occasions in 1974 when it was erroneously supposed that the Government had, in fact, changed its basic policy. The first was when the SA Ambassador to the UN told the General Assembly on 24 October that the Republic's policy was not 'inflexible', adding that 'my Government does not condone discrimination based solely on the grounds of race or colour . . . We shall do everything in our power to move away from discrimination based on race or colour . . .'. The second occasion was on 10 November when Vorster told his critics that they 'will be surprised where we will stand if SA were given "a six months' chance".' He was quick to allay suspicion in his own ranks—thereby dampening down hopes in black ranks—by explaining a few weeks later that the Government was not 'planning to allow a one-man, one-vote system in SA and, by so doing, create a multi-racial Parliament . . . That will never happen . . . It is a cardinal principle of Nationalist policy that no group dares to allow political power to slip out of its hands.' Therefore, so far as the Republic itself was concerned—irrespective of what policies it pursued in helping to promote majority rule in Rhodesia and independence in Namibia—the Grand Design of Apartheid remains the basic objective of Government policy.

The chairman of Anglo-American, Harry Oppenheimer, warned[4] that 'we are going to have a lot of trouble if detente fails'; but, as he made clear, he was speaking not only of the more obvious political consequences but because of the new labour crisis that seriously began to threaten the mines in 1974. The shortage of black labour was due, in part, to the growing reluctance among neighbouring countries to export their labour, to tribal conflicts among the migrants themselves and, above all, to the unwillingness of black South Africans to accept mine jobs under existing conditions of pay and work. To save SA's precious goose required either a continued supply of imported migrant workers at higher—but not too high—wages, or a basic restructuring of the mine labour system which would make it more attractive to SA's own labour force: but this reform could be achieved only at the cost of further eroding apartheid.

SA's defence spending continued its upward leap with the 1974–75 Budget providing a new record figure of R 702m, an increase of R 330m over the previous year, and accounting for 13.5% of total national expenditure; this compared with R 230m ten years earlier. Between 1964–65 and 1974–75 total military expenditure was R 2,864m.

Nevertheless, there were many hopeful voices in the Republic, like Laurence Gandar, the former editor-in-chief of the *Rand Daily Mail*, who spoke of 'a new era of change' having opened up for the country during 1974.[5]

The year saw some changes in apartheid laws and practices. The decision to abolish (for reasons of external pressures; see Labour Policy below) the hated Masters and Servants Act has more symbolic than practical significance; most of its provisions being either incorporated in later legislation or being in practice obsolete. The most promising change was a greater willingness to admit that Africans form a permanent part of the urban society: if translated into practice this would certainly represent a significant crack in the foundations of apartheid. In practice, however, there was no reprieve for the hundreds of thousands of African families caught up in the mass population removals felt necessary to achieve the aims of racial Separate Development.

The absurdities of apartheid were illustrated[6] by the heart surgeon, Prof Christian Barnard, who revealed that the Groote Schuur Hospital's cardiac unit is used on alternate weeks for white and black patients. 'But what happens,' he asked, 'if during a black week, a white patient needs urgent surgery. Must I tell him to wait and let him die?' Two vastly expensive cardiac units were maintained at the Robertsfield hospital—one each for whites and blacks. 'Magnificent,' said Barnard, 'except that both units could not function because there was not enough staff to keep them going. Since these were scrapped I have clandestinely established multi-racial teams—so far without protest from anyone.'

One new sign of the times was the use in the pro-Government Afrikaans Press of 'Afrikane' as the new word to describe Africans in place of the current usage of Bantu. 'Afrikane' appeared for the first time in a headline in *Die Transvaler* on 23 August 1974.

At the beginning of 1975 there was the first ominous warning from a Homeland leader of a possible new campaign of non-violent civil disobedience unless meaningful change began: this remarkable challenge came in a speech from the KwaZulu leader, Chief Gatsha Buthelezi, and is reproduced fully on page B430.

POLITICAL AFFAIRS
THE REPUBLIC'S FUTURE
Like the geese of Rome, leading citizens of all political opinions and racial communities continued their warnings about the dangers facing the Republic.[7] Few seemed to doubt the reality of the danger: they differed only about how to face it. Thus, while the Government and military leaders spoke ominously about the 'black claw of terrorism' and raised the anxiety level to a high degree (see The Mood of Afrikanerdom below), they sought at the same time to reassure the country that the Republic's military power was sufficient to ensure its defence against all its enemies and to guarantee a flourishing future. The Government and the white Opposition leaders had their different interests: either to cry havoc or to decry alarmism, depending on which audience they were appealing to.

The shock of the Portuguese experience caused leaders to revise their views about the time still available for peaceful change to occur. 'SA has one more year of grace before the cold winds from all corners of the earth blow her into rough country', wrote Wimpie de Klerk,[8] the editor of *Die Transvaler*, an official Government organ. 'It is as if everything has now come to a head . . . Our history has brought us to the crossroads, and without further procrastination we must proceed into the desert or the promised land.'

This theme of SA having reached 'a crossroads' and 'the point of no return' has already been noted in the October speech made by the Prime Minister; it was repeated throughout the year by his Ministers as well as by white and black Opposition leaders. The leader of the United Party, Sir de Villiers Graaff, speaking at the year's end, said:[9] 'The year 1974 was an important one in the history of South Africa. It will come to be seen, I believe, as a year in which we began to make a fundamental reappraisal of our situation in this sub-continent.'

Using traditional Boer symbolism, Dr J. du P. Malan said on the Day of the Covenant—which commemorates the Trekkers' victory over the Zulus in 1838—'SA is standing alone against the world as Piet Retief had stood at Blood River'. On the same day, the leader of the *verkrampte* (inward-looking) Herstigte Nasionale Party, Dr Albert Hertzog, claimed that 31 'kaffir wars' had been ended only when the white man had asserted his authority; the conditions in which those wars had taken place existed once again in southern Africa: history had shown that the black man 'could never be trusted'. But this was the extremist minority view among Afrikaner leaders. More typical was that of the Deputy Minister of Bantu Administration, Punt Janson, who warned[10] a Namibian audience that people who did not want to accept that 'the black man was busy awakening' were 'blind and irresponsible': the answer lay in establishing 'new relations' between black and white. 'But the difficulty,' warned Fred van Wyk, Director of the Institute of Race Relations, was to reverse the trend of anti-white feelings which were 'rife' among young urban Africans.[11] 'The older generation was prepared to tolerate living in a political and economic no-man's-land in the urban townships, but it is becoming clearer that the younger people desperately want change.' This danger of black urban violence was also emphasized[12] by Theo Gerdener, a former Minister of Interior and now leader of the Democratic Party. With the ending of the wars in Vietnam and the Portuguese territories, arms from Communist countries for 'crude terrorist attacks on civilian institutions' would be diverted to SA, he warned. This threat could be countered only by whites standing against their common enemies and by greater co-operation between South Africa, Rhodesia and other countries in southern Africa—black and white. 'No white minority in southern Africa,' he added 'could any longer remain standing on its own . . . I have warned that whites who believe that white supremacy can be maintained for ever must think again.'

The new Afrikaner voice in the Progressive Party, Dr F. van Zyl Slabbert, MP, warned[13] that in the last analysis it was the judgement of black SA which would decide whether there was to be violent conflict or co-operation in the Republic, adding: 'To me, it is abundantly clear that any nation which attempts to preserve its identity by discriminating against others creates the historical circumstances for its own destruction. It is a tortuous logic that argues that you can prevent friction between people by discriminating between them. But how can an Opposition attack the Government on this if they are themselves victims of the same disease?'

A radical attack on traditional SA ideas was made by the Judge President of the Cape Division, Mr Justice Andrew Brink Beyers, on his retirement from the Bench. In an interview with the *Sunday Times* (10 March 1974) he said that while the 'civilized' must continue to rule, 'the civilized cannot be judged by the colour of his skin'. While he was not a democrat, he said that rulers should be chosen purely on merit. He described the policy of the Homelands as 'a stupid concept', adding that 'the only good that has come out of it is the creation of black leaders—the last thing the Government wanted'. He was pessimistic about the future because he said he did not believe that the right policies would be adopted 'because whites would not give up their privileged position'.

The military leaders led the chorus of warnings about the coming struggle against armed insurgents. The head of the army, Lt-Gen. Magnus Malan, warned[14] that the country's 'crisis ceiling' was very low; the slightest incident could land SA in a crisis of international proportions. 'For example, a terrorist's success, or even a meaningful terrorist action, could lead to SA's enemies giving more help to the terrorists, and that would increase the international standing of the terrorist.'

'The black claw of terrorism has already hit the whole of SA,' the Minister of Police, Jimmy Kruger, declared[15] at the gravestone of an 18-year-old policeman killed in Rhodesia. It was, he added, 'probably the twentieth time' he had already stood beside the open grave of a young South African killed in fighting guerrillas; but 'each grave of a terrorist victim will be a monument to SA's future'.

While the military leaders and the Ministers spoke optimistically of the growing ability of the Republic's armed forces to withstand any attack, white burghers and their wives were encouraged to form Home Guards in towns and villages throughout the country. At a meeting to start such a unit in Naboomspruit, the mayor said the country was 'preparing for war'. The local commanding officer, referring to what had happened in Mozambique, commented:[16] 'Something has happened close to us which shows that the threat to our country has now arrived on our back step.'

Among the very few voices who spoke of the dangers of creating 'a war psychosis' was the Progressive Party Leader, Colin Eglin. But in the view of the Minister of Interior, Dr Connie Mulder, 'the Government of South Africa can never be too strong, because the real Opposition is the world outside.'[17] Significantly he added that the Government was 'kept up to the mark by security threats'.

Reactions to the Portuguese abdication in Mozambique were of two kinds: those who saw it as bringing the violence closer to the Republic, thus increasing the importance of military preparedness; and those who argued that the violent confrontation could be stemmed only by finding political solutions. Arguing this second point, John Barratt, director of the SA Institute of Race Relations, wrote[18] that neither greater military power nor more economic concessions would solve the problem. 'The Portuguese experience has shown again that this kind of "liberation" conflict cannot be settled by military means. This is basically not a military question, but rather a political one, in which all the people are involved.'

The country's industrial leaders were prominent among those who warned of the need for quick change if disaster was to be avoided. Addressing a trade union conference, the President of the Chamber of Mines, R. A. Plumbridge, spoke 'hopefully' of change by 'mutual agreement, discussion and evolution; but, at any rate, change—and at a quickening tempo.' Accepting the certainty of 'a period of industrial unrest, Harry Oppenheimer warned:[19] Unless the representation of black workers for discussion and negotiation with management is radically and rapidly improved, that unrest is going to have very serious consequences indeed.'

'Black workers could not understand why rights extended to other workers did not apply to them as well,' Alex Boraine, the new Progressive Party MP and labour consultant to the Anglo-American Corporation, told a conference of the Institute of Personnel Management.[20] He warned: 'We must consider the realities—and the reality is not only white fear but also black anger.'

On the black side, however, the warnings were all about the failure to move quickly enough. Chief Lucas Mangope, Chief Minister of BophuthaTswana warned[21] that 'time is running out for the white man to come to terms with the growing awareness and impatience of the black man in SA'. He added that the next five years looked like being 'a neck and neck race between the black man's impatience and the white man's capacity and willingness to rally his spiritual, political and economic resources'. Once again the sharpest challenge came from Chief Gatsha Buthelezi, who warned the Prime Minister that nobody should be left in any doubt about 'civil disobedience and disruption of services as a logical alternative to meaningful changes in SA's race policies'.[22]

There were many warnings from outside the country as well. Testifying to the African sub-committee of the Congress Foreign Affairs Committee, Donald Easum, the US Assistant Secretary of State for African Affairs said[23] that a week he had spent in SA was a 'sobering experience'. He went on to say that the old *status quo* in SA was crumbling and that 'it is in SA's own interest to encourage early and orderly movement towards settlement in both Rhodesia and Namibia'.

POLITICAL AFFAIRS
THE 1974 ELECTIONS
In the general election held in April the ruling party won an overwhelming mandate from the exclusively white electorate to continue its policies of apartheid. It won two more seats to command 122 of Parliament's 171 members, and more than wiped out the losses recorded in 1970.[24] It also further reduced the vote of the splinter *verkrampte* Herstigte Nasionale Party, which won no seats and lost most of its deposits. The official Opposition, the United Party, shed votes to the ruling party and seats to the Progressive Party which, alone among the Opposition, succeeded in improving its position—from one to seven. In a subsequent by-election in Pinelands (Cape Province) it captured an eighth seat.

RESULTS OF 1974 ELECTIONS

	NP	UP	PP	Totals
Transvaal	61(58)	11(14)	4(1)	76(73)
Cape	37(36)	15(18)	3(—)	55(54)
Natal	5 (3)	15(15)	—(—)	20(18)
OFS	14(15)	—(—)	—(—)	14(15)
SWA	6 (6)	—(—)	—(—)	6 (6)

Figures in brackets represent the number of seats held in the previous Parliament.

	No of seats contested	Average no of votes per seat contested	Percentage of total vote*
National Party	136	4,695	56.2
United Party	111	3,278	32.0
Progressive Party	22	3,290	6.4
Herstigte Nasionale Party	50	884	3.9
Democratic Party	8	1,592	1.1
Others and independents	11	343	0.4

* In its issue of 3 May the *South African Digest* gave slighly different figures for the percentage of total votes cast gained by the various parties, *viz* NP 57.2, UP 32.7, PP 5.3, HNP 3.6, DP 0.9, others and independents 0.4.

GOVERNMENT CHANGES
The Cabinet was changed in February 1975 when the Minister of Finance, Dr Nicolas Diederichs, became the new State President in place of J. J. Fouche. The new Minister of Finance, Senator Owen Horwood, is the only English-speaking member of the Government. He is a former professor and brother-in-law of Rhodesia's Ian Smith. Chris Heunis took Horwood's place as Minister of Economic Affairs. The leading *verligte* in the Cabinet, Dr Koornhof, earlier had Mines and Immigration added to his portfolio as Minister of Sport. Vorster introduced Marais Steyn as the new Minister of Tourism and Indian Affairs. Steyn had defected from the UP front-bench as late as 1973; and during his 25 previous years in Parliament he had been one of the sharpest critics of apartheid: the man who only a short time before could say that 'this is the worst Government that God has cursed this country with', became one of its Ministers.

THE FEDERAL ISSUE

The pursuit of federalism[25] as a constitutional solution to SA's racial problems continued to divide the Republic's politicians during 1974. The Government decided to make federation a crucial issue by suggesting that the general election offered voters a choice between Separate Development—with its promise of 'independent black and white States'—and a multi-racial federation. The UP continued to advocate a multi-racial federation of separate States with separate voters' rolls for each race, whose representatives would sit together in a Federal Assembly. The Progressives advocated a Federal Parliament elected on common voters' rolls, but with a weighted Senate, and an entrenched Bill of Rights to prevent any race dominating the others. However, during 1974 the Progressives decided to appoint a new commission to re-examine its constitutional proposals.

The black leaders of the Homelands (except for Chief Wessels Motha of the tiny Basotho Qwaqwa) continued to support a long-term federal solution. However, Chief Kaiser Matanzima of the Transkei disagreed with the other six Homeland leaders in favouring the creation of a federation only after the Homelands had become independent; the rest favour federation before independence. A joint statement[26] by the Homeland leaders (except for Basotho Qwaqwa's, but including the Transkei's) affirmed their belief that 'at this point of time, when SA is at the crossroads, the concept of federation needs attention as one of the possible alternatives worth looking at'.

Critics of federalism continued to attack it during the year from two opposing directions. Speaking for the Left, the Indian sociologist, Fatima Meer, declared:[27] 'Federation is the rhetoric of the moment. Africans who propose it do so partly to reassure whites that they do not intend to overpower them, and partly to reassure themselves that they can effect inter-tribal unity and realize African nationalism. Whites propose it to reaffirm the racist conspiracy established against blacks by the Act of Union . . . However expressed, and whatever the apparent hopes that presently motivate it, it is, in the final analysis, the non-Nationalist seal to apartheid. Its present currency is hardly inspired by the genuine belief in its constitutional superiority over Union: it is provoked by a surrender to apartheid and a need to come to terms with it. It is an attempt to solve race through racism and therein lies its bankruptcy.'

Prof. Nic Rhoodie,[28] followed a similar line of criticism; he claimed that in the light of the power struggle in the country a federation could provide only a temporary solution since it would not permanently satisfy black aspirations. His own alternative solution was that of a Commonwealth of States—which is what the ruling party stands for. His main argument was that: 'Considering the pronounced differences between the established politico-historical groups in SA, Separate Development commonwealth-style may well become the political catalyst in the sub-continent capable of creating a constellation of economically interdependent but freely interacting political units, without forever preventing the peoples concerned from negotiating forms of co-operation and accommodation that will harmonize with their adaptive needs.'

CORRUPTION

Allegations of corruption in SA's public life continue to upset the Government. The Minister of Economic Affairs promised early legislation to curb 'unsubstantiated allegations of corruption against officials'. Earlier, an Opposition Senator had alleged[29] that there were irregularities involving members of the Cabinet and top officials, including one which 'contains the classic elements of Watergate'. Senator Monty Crook—who had exposed the Faroes Affair involving corruption in the Railways, which led to the jailing of three top Government officials and a shipping director—made fresh allegations[30] 'worse than the Faroes Affair' over land deals involving sales to a parastatal corporation, Iscor. Iscor at once ordered an investigation. The Government rejected demands in Parliament to investigate other land deals involving Iscor's huge new development scheme in Saldanha Bay. Another State organization, the Bantu Investment Corporation, was the subject of considerable Parliamentary discussion; after an investigation one top official resigned, the twelfth to do so in four years. But Progressive Party MPs continued to demand a proper commission of inquiry into BIC's affairs. The Nationalist-dominated Cape Administration was accused by Theo Aronson MP of 'covering up' a report into the Wavecrest Affair which, he alleged, might eventually involve over £600m—'the worst scandal that has happened since the Nationalist Party assumed office in 1948'.[31]

After the Faroes—which the Government had initially refused to investigate—the general manager of SA Railways admitted[32] that 'the damage done to us by the Faroes shipping disclosures, and now the evidence of corruption in the sale of our scrap material, has put a question mark over the Railways'. The *Rand Daily Mail* agreed to hand over a complete dossier it had received in what was described as the Pasternoster 'Fishing Affair' after a judicial commission of inquiry was promised. Fred Barnard, the late Prime Minister, Dr Verwoerd's, private secretary for 13 years, appeared in court in October 1974 on charges of bribery, alternatively corruption.

THE ROLE OF THE PRIME MINISTER

After eight years as Prime Minister, John Balthazzar Vorster finally succeeded in establishing the complete authority of the ruling party as a result of his electoral victory. He succeeded in getting control over the *Broederbond*, the secret society which co-ordinates the ramified cultural, economic, religious, social and political organizations of the Afrikaners (see below). Having moved in a rightward direction in 1973[33] to protect his flank from the *verkramptes* (the inward-looking and narrow-minded conservatives), he could again return more confidently to a more *verligte* (enlightened, outward-looking) pragmatism. He was strong enough to pursue detente with Black Africa and to make further concessions towards the objective of lessening racial discrimination in sport. (See below.) He began to edge towards granting independence (albeit his own version of that concept) to Namibia (see previous chapter) and adopted a muted but unmistakable policy of advocating black majority rule for Rhodesia. At home he moved more urgently towards encouraging Bantustan leaders to claim the independence for the Homelands he was offering them; but he refused concessions to the Coloureds. He was more willing, however, to take risks with his own *verkramptes* over proposals to get rid of 'petty apartheid'—the minor irritants of discrimination—and he became the first Prime Minister to engage in regular consultations with black leaders. But, as he repeatedly declared, none of his policy changes should be seen as any weakening on his part of a determination to maintain white rule over that four-fifths of the country designated exclusively for white ownership and political control.

In the context of Afrikanerdom, Vorster was running up the flag of compromise; but this was not the way the Republic's black majority saw it. None the less, Vorster's policy inevitably split his party between the ultra-conservatives and the more flexible conservatives. The significance of this policy was explained by one of the veteran Afrikaner writers, Schalk Pienaar, the editor-in-chief of the pro-Government *Beeld*:[34] At the heart of the National Party were two difficult, irreconcilable viewpoints: the one accepted the theory that races in SA could be separated, and the other 'practically accepted' that they could not; the Government recognized the existence of these two viewpoints among its supporters and tried to accommodate both; but this was extremely difficult, if not impossible, to do and led to all kinds of ambiguities. How long, he asked, could the confrontation between these two irreconcilable viewpoints be put off; if there was to be confrontation, was it not better that it should occur sooner rather than later? His conclusion was that Vorster needed public support for his policies to succeed so that he could be 'free to deal with the new international and internal problems'.

The need to split the ruling party—traditionally regarded as a cardinal sin by the ranks of Afrikanerdom—found other advocates as well. J. J. Van Tonder, a senior lecturer in political science at Potchefstroom University, asked[35] whether there was still a place in the ruling party for the 'political brakemen and obstruction-ists' (the *verkramptes*); should they not be eliminated in the same way as had happened with the minority of *verkramptes* who were forced to leave the National Party in 1969?[36] Dirk Richard, editor of the pro-government *Die Vaderland* prédicted[37] that Vorster would have to depart from some aspects of 'traditional' Afrikaner Nationalist thinking. 'It will surprise me if the National Party remains for long the same as they are today. But the National Party will remain the centre.' The political boundaries would have to change to place outside them those now inside the ruling party and to bring in others who were now outside. Thus Vorster was in practice being cast in the new role of the leader of an emerging coalition between *verligte* Afrikaners and the right-wing of the Opposition.

These ideas were also echoed in the Opposition camp where there were growing demands for a realignment of forces. 'Not since the Progressives broke away from the United Party in 1959 has there been such a strong desire for a realignment of all *verligtes* in the Opposition as now,' wrote Hans Strydom, one of the best-informed political writers in the country.[38] Vorster's former Minister of Interior, Theo Gerdener, advocated a summit meeting to bring together all the *verligte* politicians to 'break what many of them consider to be an explosive dead-lock in the country's race problems'.[39]

Vorster summed up[40] his own position in the changing political situation: politics, he said, was no longer the 'art of the possible' but the art of reconciling conflicting interests; Separate Development had reached the point where nobody could any longer undo what had been done; most people believed in the idea of Separate Development.

PARLIAMENTARY PARTIES
HERENIGDE NASIONALE PARTY (NP)

The Prime Minister's policy of challenging the *verkramptes* in his own ranks produced a series of crises in the Parliamentary caucas and in the Cabinet. The sharpest and most persistent conflict, interestingly enough, was over the country's policy on sport—a reflection of SA's concern over the success of the international sports boycott. A second divisive issue was that of the future place of the Coloured community in the social and political system—an issue on which Vorster, while making some concessions, took a hard line against his own *verligtes*. A third contentious issue was over control of the *Broederbond* (see below); a fourth was over the growing confrontation with the Afrikaner intelligentsia who strongly opposed Government proposals for internal censorship (see below). But, perhaps, the most explosive was over Vorster's apparent willingness to persuade the Smith regime to accept the inevitability of black majority rule for Rhodesia (see Foreign Affairs below).

The Government was divided not only about these issues but also over the rivalries for the succession to the Prime Ministership. The *verkrampte* leadership in the ruling

24

party stayed with Dr Andries Treurnicht[41] whose real sympathies lie with the breakaway Herstigte Nasionale Party. Vorster moved toughly to ensure his defeat as chairman of the *Broederbond* (see below). Treurnicht's strongest Cabinet ally was Dr Connie Mulder, the chairman of the Transvaal Nationalists who had been looked upon as Vorster's natural successor;[42] but Mulder's stocks appeared to be slipping. His style of leadership was in the familiar Boer mould of *kragdadigheid* (unyielding strength); but in the circumstances of 1974 there appeared to be less appeal for Afrikaners in this uncompromisingly tough and, at times, crude attitude. Mulder was cautioned by one of the pro-Government papers, *Die Vaderland*,[43] that *kragdadigheid* was an advantage of past leaders; in the new delicate situation the qualities of pragmatism and diplomacy were to be preferred. The paper warned him that unless he was more careful in future in handling critical issues—such as the future of the Coloured community—he would be resisted by the Afrikaans Press in the same way as had happened with the *verkramptes* in 1969. His three rivals for succession appeared to be the Minister of Defence, P. W. Botha, leader of the Cape Nationalists; Dr Piet Koornhof, the Minister of Sport, perhaps the most enlightened of the younger Nationalists in Government; and Fanie Botha, the Minister of Water Affairs and Irrigation. There were reports[44] in September that Connie Mulder and Treurnicht were involved in secret talks to form a new right-wing front within the Government. These moves led the editor of *Die Transvaler*, Dr Wimpie de Klerk, to take the unusual action of writing about internal Government conflicts. An article headed 'Mr Vorster and the Backstabbers',[45] while not mentioning them by name, left little doubt that Mulder and Treurnicht were the principal targets. 'They hide behind wishful thinking,' de Klerk wrote, 'that changes on certain levels can be stopped. They whisper around that principles are being raped.' The country, he added, could not afford to have its political leader undermined in this way. Another pro-Government paper, *Rapport*, wrote[46] about the conflict between the Cabinet and the younger Afrikaner intelligentsia over censorship (see Afrikaners below); it confirmed that other issues causing divisions inside the Government caucas were over Coloured policy, so-called 'petty apartheid', sport and the leadership struggle within the *Broederbond*.

The confrontation over sport came to a head in the HNP Parliamentary caucas on 2 September when Koornhof and Treurnicht clashed strongly over a speech made by a new Nationalist MP, Dawie de Villiers, the former Springbok rugby captain, calling for national rugby and cricket teams to be chosen on merit. The controversy raged until March 1975 when, faced with a threat by the French to cancel their rugby tour and the Australians to cancel their cricket tour, the Cabinet agreed that one match could be played against the French by a 'multi-national' (not multi-racial) team, and that a similarly mixed team could play against a visiting English cricket XI. But there was to be no joint practice games between the races to decide the merit of players. Having gone this far in denting the rigid colour bar in sport, the Government still insisted that the policy on sport had remained 'unchanged': multi-racialism was out; multi-nationalism, consistent with Separate Development, was permissible.

HERSTIGTE NASIONALE PARTY (HNP)

The Herstigtes, formed after the breakaway from the National Party in 1969, failed to make progress in the April elections, winning only 3.9% of the vote in the 50 constituencies they contested. Nevertheless, under their leader, Dr Albert Hertzog, they continued to polarize Afrikaner opinion between their *verkrampte* outlook—which insists on national unity based on the core of Afrikanerdom and on Afrikaans as the national language—and the brand of *verligte* policies advocated by

Vorster. Their past stronghold was in the *Broederbond*, but there, too, they seemed to have suffered a setback in the 1974 elections of office-bearers (see *Broederbond* below). Nor did they succeed in making a success of the Volkskongress held in September when only 200 delegates attended instead of the expected 700. But shrewd political commentators still warned against underestimating the potential strength of this white backlash party in the difficult days of white-black confrontation ahead.

UNITED PARTY (UP)

The official Opposition party fared badly in the elections, losing six of its 47 seats and winning only 32% of the total vote. It was riven by dissensions between its more liberal and conservative wings, with the liberals gaining a fresh access of blood through younger MPs in the elections. The party leader, Sir de Villiers Graaff, attempted to lessen the internal dissensions and to fight off the challenge of the Progressive Party by adopting forward-looking policies. During 1974 it was agreed that party policy should aim at the removal within a federal framework of colour discrimination; that the Immorality Act should be re-examined; and that Job Reservation should be rejected. It accepted compulsory education for all races and the right of Africans to become part of multi-racial trade unions. It also agreed to accept the principle, if both communities desired it, for whites and Coloureds to 'merge their rights and interests'. But these concessions only served to deepen the cleavage between the two sections of the party. The internal crisis came to a head in February 1975. Ten members of the Transvaal Provincial Council, supporters of the UP's progressive leader, Harry Schwarz, MP, resigned from the UP to form the Reform Party. They said they no longer felt the UP 'is the vehicle in which we can travel the path of *verligtheid*'. Schwarz and four other MPs resigned from the caucas to reduce the UP's strength in Parliament to 36. Although closer to the Progressives, the new Reform Party made no immediate move to merge the two parties which would give them a bloc of 12 seats in Parliament.

PROGRESSIVE PARTY (PP)

The PP, which broke away from the UP under the leadership of Mrs Helen Suzman in 1959, made considerable headway in the elections by winning six seats and later capturing another in a by-election. Its formidable leader, who had battled alone as the party's representative in Parliament for 15 years, gained a number of outstanding young colleagues, including the PP leader, Colin Eglin; two distinguished Afrikaners—Renier de Villiers, former editor of *The Star* and a cousin of Leo Marquard (who died during 1974), and Prof. F. van Zyl Slabbert; and two young executives of Harry Oppenheimer's Anglo-American Corporation—his former son-in-law and Scottish rugby international player, Gordon Waddell, and Dr Alex Boraine, a Methodist lay preacher and expert in labour affairs. The PP fought a number of Parliamentary battles in support of its principles which accept that SA is a multi-racial country whose citizens are interdependent; that merit, not colour, should count; that the right constitution for the country is a federal State consisting of largely autonomous provinces; that all discriminatory laws should be rescinded; and that a Bill of Rights should be entrenched in the constitution.

DEMOCRATIC PARTY (DP)

The DP, which was formed in 1973 after its leader, Theo Gerdener, resigned as Minister of Interior,[47] managed to put up only eight candidates in the elections and attracted 1.1% of the total vote. It is opposed to the maintenance of white supremacy and favours a twin-stream policy—with whites, Coloureds and Indians gradually achieving equal rights in one stream, and Africans achieving full political and social rights in the second stream within Homelands; but borders would have to be redrawn to make these viable and completely independent States. The two streams would, in time, merge to form a confederation. The party's main role continued to be that of a catalyst seeking to bring about a new coalition of enlightened parties in opposition to the ruling party.

VERLIGTE ACTION
This is a movement and not a political party which was launched in 1973[48] to promote the need for enlightened action among intellectuals of all races. It has the support of leaders of the radical Black Sash organization, Progressives and Democratic Party. It suffered the defection of some of its leaders during 1974 but made some progress in establishing a multi-racial executive committee. Its objective is to pursue the ideal of a society that will recognize the dignity of all its people.

THE MOOD OF AFRIKANERDOM
The Afrikaners' self-questioning about the success of apartheid and their future on the African continent appeared less confident that in previous years in the public debate conducted among themselves.[49] An unusual number of Afrikanerdom's 'Old Guard' intellectuals spoke critically of the failure of past policies and of the 'need for change'. But was the Afrikaner willing to change fast enough? This question was posed by Prof. J. D. Van der Vywer, dean of the Faculty of Law at the University of Potchefstroom in the December 1974 issue of *Woord en Daad*, the journal of the Afrikaans Calvinist Society. The analysis of the Republic's race problems offered from the seat of Afrikanerdom was little different from what had been said for years, but only in liberal circles. 'South Africa may as well admit to itself, and confess in front of the world that the present state of the SA law and social structure entails racial discrimination and promotes injustice . . . ' he wrote. 'Particularly with the Afrikaner there is an increasing realization and acceptance of the fact that apartheid, in the sense of racially-based segregationary practices in the everyday social intercourse, dare not and cannot be the omega of the SA pattern of life . . . Afrikaners, particularly, still did not want to accept the relinquishing of part of the fatherland to blacks. I doubt if we are going to be granted another ten years to get our house in order.'

Another Establishment figure, the veteran editor and political writer, Willem van Heerden, spoke of the failure to adopt 'new ways of thinking'[50] and, more significantly, criticized the use of coercion 'to achieve political and even religious aims'. He added that 'our present policy to force people apart in spheres where they want to be together can have the effect of making us the recluse of the world. It may also cause a reaction among ourselves which may defeat the object of survival instead of promoting it.' He described the policy of 'parallel development' for Coloureds as 'outmoded'. The Homeland concept, he admitted, was 'no longer the alpha and omega of a settlement' between the races; and he exposed the failure of most of the racial policies outlined by Dr Verwoerd 15 years ago—which, incidentally, he had supported at the time.

Opposing demands for radical rethinking of fundamental policies were a group of leading Afrikaner intellectuals who felt that the need was only to define 'more clearly and more honestly' the policies of Separate Development. Thus Dr R. R. Tusenius, director of the Stellenbosch Postgraduate School of Management argued[51] that after the splitting of the races, which had occurred in the earlier phases of implementing Separate Development, 'in this phase it is now urgently necessary to define as quickly as possible clear objectives and implementation of tables'. He described the present phase as comprising parallel, multi-national development, separate

27

freedoms, Homelands for blacks with their franchise there, and contact with black States.

Despite views of Afrikaner intellectuals like Dr Tusenius, Prof. Nic Olivier—a former leading figure in the SA Bureau of Racial Affairs (the Afrikaner intellectuals' think-tank) and now a United Party MP—felt that there were positive indications of 'new thinking' in the ruling party.[52] He thought this could be developed through a combination of international pressures and an awareness of bitterness among black South Africans. Although he cited a number of changes, he agreed they were peripheral to the central issues; nevertheless, they did show 'the Government's growing sensitivity to the needs of our black communities'. However, in spite of the new trends of thinking among Afrikaners, he saw, as yet, 'no indication that the Government are prepared to reconsider their ideologies and policies in any fundamental way'.

While some Afrikaner leaders were willing to admit—as did the Minister of Interior, Dr Connie Mulder on one occasion[53]—that 'SA society was far from perfect', he and others nevertheless insisted that the Republic was a happy country. 'Look at our peoples—all of them,' Dr Mulder told a student audience,[54] 'Look into their smiling, untroubled faces and understand what we are trying to achieve in the field of human relations.' This was also the message of the State President, J. J. Fouche, who declared:[55] 'We confirm that the security, prosperity and peace which we desire for ourselves we also grant with open heart to every other citizen—white, brown and black—who wishes to share this country and its gifts with us in peace and friendship.'

How much real change has there been among young Afrikaners in recent years? What is the explanation for the contradictions reflected in their attitudes? Two major studies published in 1974 threw some light on both these questions. A survey of Afrikaner attitudes[56] by Prof. Lawrence Schlemmer of the Natal Institute of Social Research showed that, on the whole, there was little significant difference between the attitudes of young Afrikaners between the age of 16 to 24 years and the older generation on most issues affecting race. This younger group was shown to include a higher than average proportion of people with conservative attitudes. The only significant differences between younger and older people was over their attitude to whether Africans will ever have 'the abilities of whites'. In the 16–24 age group, 57% thought they would never have the abilities of whites as against 55% in the 25–34 age group, 62% in the 35–42 age group, and 69% in the over 55 age group. Over the crucial question of whether whites should pay higher taxes to assist black development 97% of the youngest group (the same number as for the over 55s) and 99% of the 25–34 age group were against. The same survey asked white South Africans what they would do if 'it seemed that blacks would come to power'. Almost an equal number of English (18%) and Afrikaans-speaking (19%) people said they would leave, while 23% and 22% respectively said they would 'think of leaving': thus 41% of both white communities took the same attitude. Asked what they would do if the standard of living dropped, only 4% of Afrikaners said they would definitely leave and 15% would think of leaving, as against 8% and 19% respectively among the English. The voting pattern of Afrikaners has not changed significantly in recent years: for the United Party support has remained at under c. 10%, and for the Progressive under 1%. Younger Afrikaners' (16–24) support for both these Opposition parties is only 1% above the average for all Afrikaner age-groups. Schlemmer's tentative conclusion is that 'the profile of attitudes which seems to be characteristic of 16-24-year-old Afrikaners offers scant encouragement to those who hope for more enlightened and forward-looking race policies, whether along the lines of separate Development or that of the common society.'

The other survey of white attitudes was carried out by Dr H. I. J. van der Spuy, an Afrikaner psychiatrist (who recently emigrated with his family to Canada) for a book entitled *The Psychodynamics of Apartheid*. In lectures he gave and articles he published[57] van der Spuy said that all the evidence pointed to white South Africans being more neurotic than most other national groups in the world for whom comparable criteria are available. One of his conclusions is that the independent criteria for 'the obsessional personality' applied to many of the practices of the SA Government. 'The obsessional personality is among others noted for his 'conscientiousness and love of order and discipline; its persistence and endurance even in the face of obstacles . . . he is difficult to move, but set moving in a given direction persists in it and is difficult to stop or deflect . . . finds himself most at home in a world in which all is ordered . . . The love of order and discipline is extended to others; and obsessional people tend to be strict parents and domineering masters' . . . An obsessional outlook on life, in combination with an authoritarian personality, a belief that Government authority is divinely sanctioned, a paternalistic attitude towards blacks, a simplistic view of blacks as emotionally and intellectually on the level of children and a good dosage of old school dogmatic Calvinistic theology culminates in a view of apartheid in all its facets as an entirely morally justified system, fully supported by Christian ethics.' Van der Spuy also identified the 'obsessional' and 'authoritarian' personality of the Afrikaner ruling establishment, and spoke of their 'feeling of national persecution: the belief that there is some sort of international plot against Afrikaners'. He commented that 'as is usual with ideas of persecution in its clinical manifestation, it is also in this case (the Afrikaner ruling Establishment) coupled with ideas of grandeur—the proclamation of 'a divine purpose' in the Afrikaners' history.

All these traits of obsession, authoritarianism, grandeur and national persecution came out most strongly in the speeches made at the Volkskongress (see above) organized by the *verkramptes* who, in this sense, can be labelled with scientific objectivity as the 'lunatic fringe' of the obsessional society of Afrikanerdom. In order to fulfill his 'calling in an unfettered way', the Afrikaner nation 'needs to be free', according to Dr C. J. Jooste, the director of the Government-supported SA Bureau of Racial Affairs.[58] He added: 'The Afrikaner must have exclusive control over his State and he must be able to decide exclusively over his geographic area and his resources.'

AFRIKANER INTELLIGENTSIA

The growing confrontation between the Government and the sophisticated younger Afrikaner writers and academics produced a critical debate in the ruling party's Parliamentary caucus in October (see above). The immediate issue was over the bitterly contested law enacted by Parliament to tighten internal censorship which followed the banning for the first time of an Afrikaans book—Andre Brink's *Kennis van die Aand*. The target of the Afrikaans writers' campaign was the Minister of Interior, Dr Connie Mulder, who had piloted the Bill through Parliament. According to the pro-Government *Rapport*,[59] virtually all the leading Afrikaans writers 'are in revolt' against the Act. The paper commented editorially that, while differences of opinion would always occur, 'but alienation between writers and the Government is at present too great to be healthy'.

Breyten Breytenbach, faced with a request from his publisher to accept self-censorship, called on Afrikaans writers to go underground rather than to submit to self-censorship which, he said,[60] was already very strong in the Afrikaans literary world. Another Afrikaans writer, Jan Rabie, also refused to censor his new book *Ark*, the theme of which is the survival of the Afrikaners. He described[61] the Censorship Act as 'one of the two most anti-Afrikaans laws yet enacted'—the other being their action in 'banning the Coloured people into limbo'. He added: 'The shadow of self-censorship is there and all I can say is "God help us".'

The pressures against the Afrikaner intellectuals in the Christian Institute were kept up.[62] Its leader, Dr C. F. Beyers Naude, whose passport was withdrawn, was named as the 1974 winner of the Reinhold Niebuhr award for his 'steadfast and self-sacrificing services in SA for justice and peace'.

The children of a number of prominent Afrikaners actively opposed their parents. Mrs Elsa Semmelink, the daughter of the *Broederbond*'s former chairman, Dr Andries Treurnicht, worked against the ruling party in the general election.[63] The son of a Nationalist MP, G. du Plessis, publicly campaigned for 'political integration between Coloureds and whites', even though he is himself a member of the ruling party's youth wing. Miss Antoinette de Villiers, the daughter of a *Broederbonder*, applied for political asylum in Britain after 'a long fight with my conscience in SA . . . I got out of SA because my position there became intolerable . . . I began to loathe its way of life.'[64]

THE BROEDERBOND

The power struggle between the *verligtes* and *verkramptes* for control over the secret society[65]—which co-ordinates the Afrikaner political, social, cultural, religious and economic organizations—produced another major victory for the enlightened wing of the ruling party. Having earlier expelled Dr Albert Hertzog, the HNP leader, for disclosing its secrets, the *broeders* rejected their chairman, Dr Andries Treurnicht (see above) in favour of Vorster's candidate, Prof. Gerrit Viljoen, rector of the Rand Afrikaans University. Treurnicht withdrew from the contest in October once it was clear that he could not hope to win. In September, Vorster had summoned a secret emergency meeting of the *Broederbond*'s top body to demand support for his policies on sport and the Coloureds (see above) against Treurnicht's sharp challenge.[66] Treurnicht's defeat was the result of intensive lobbying by Vorster's supporters including, according to one source,[67] the Bureau of State Security (BOSS) and the Security Police. Treurnicht then refused to stand for the executive committee. The Minister of Interior, Dr Connie Mulder, who was identified with some of Treurnicht's policies, also refused to continue as an executive member. The publicity given to these rivalries within the once notoriously secret society had the effect of bringing its activities more into the open. Once never discussed in the Afrikaans Press, several pro-Government organs[68] invited the *Broederbond* to shed its 'secrecy and mysteriousness' and to 'come into the sun'.

THE AFRICAN MOOD

To use a Stock Exchange phrase—'Kaffirs are lively'; they became even more so in 1975. Black industrial leaders, feeling the tide swinging in their favour, took more militant attitudes over trade union and other industrial rights; Homeland leaders spoke out more boldly; black student leaders, though under heavy police pressure, remained defiant; urban leaders became more vociferous. The collapse of Portuguese colonialism and the Prime Minister's search for detente with Black Africa brought confrontation between black and white to a new pitch—not yet violent but threatening. Black SA leaders warned that detente with Black Africa would be meaningless unless it began at home; this warning was given collectively by the Homeland leaders in their talks with the Prime Minister in January 1975.

Prof. Hudson Ntsanwisi, Chief Minister of Gazankulu, told a Progressive Party congress in July that it would be 'unrealistic and naive to minimize the extent to which the success of movements outside SA's borders are capturing the imagination of many black people'. Prof. Ntsanwisi was one of three Homeland leaders to support an invitation issued by the SA Students Organization (Saso) to Frelimo leaders to visit the Republic. Stressing that his own Shangaan people have common ties of blood and history, and a common language, (Tsonga), with the Shangaans of Mozambique, Ntsanwisi added: 'Frelimo is a fact; it wields power and, if we are wise, we will settle down and talk to its leaders.' Dr Cedric Phatudi, Chief Minister of Lebowá, believed that exchanges with Frelimo leaders would be beneficial and he hoped they would recognize the value of relations with the Homeland leaders. The third leader to welcome a dialogue with Frelimo was Chief Lucas Mangope, the Chief Minister of BophuthaTswana.

Dialogue between blacks and whites was no longer just a vogue; it had become commonplace. The Prime Minister himself led the consultations with Homeland leaders, and black leaders were invited to all the Opposition parties' conferences. But dialogue began to develop a more rasping note. Addressing a United Party meeting, Father Smangaliso Mkhatshwa commented:[69] 'I believe if any black person has anything worthwhile to say, he had better say it to his own people. There is nothing that depresses me so much as seeing some of our so-called Bantustan leaders spending most of their speaking time on multi-racial platforms. After the white man has been avoiding the black man like a leper for about 400 years, blacks can be excused if they regard this sudden proliferation of multi-racial meetings with some suspicion. Your biggest task is to prepare SA for the new society among your own people.'

This was the kind of remark white audiences might have expected from a Saso militant, not from a secretary of the Catholic Bishops Conference. Equally unexpected was the sharp criticism of a black pastor of the Dutch Reformed Church, the Rev. E. M. Thema, who told a white audience at a Verligte Action meeting not to suppose that urban blacks were satisfied with their lot.[70] 'The black man is placed in a position where he cannot speak his mind for fear of being branded an agitator.' To commit urban Africans to the Homelands' policy, he went on, was 'an offence to their humanity'—a policy which, any way, 'can never be fulfilled'. To continue removing them to Homelands was to degrade the territories to the status of 'perfect dumping grounds for human flesh'. And to try and divide Africans into ethnic groups was abhorrent. Another black Christian, Dr Manaz Buthelezi of the Christian Institute, said[71] that 'no self-respecting black believes that only the white man is equipped to safeguard Western civilization and Christian tradition. The black man and the white man stand to lose from the perpetuation of this myth.' The Church, said Saso in a statement to *Ecunews*, the bulletin of the SA Council of Churches, is felt by black youth to have aligned itself with the *status quo* in that it has for too long contributed to 'the dehumanization of blacks and to the corruption of the Biblical message . . . , In this way the Church becomes an accomplice of black oppression'.

Saso also helped to organize a Sharpeville remembrance day in Soweto on 22 March, where the former president of the ANC, Mrs Lillian Ngoyi, who had been under banning orders for 11 years, declared: 'We are here lest we forget . . . the torch of freedom burns on. No amount of house arrests and bannings will stop the march of freedom.' The PAC organizer of the campaign that led to Sharpeville, Robert Mangaliso Sobukwe,[72] was still under restriction in Kimberley, where he was visited in November 1974 by two black Americans—the tennis player, Arthur Ashe, and Martin Luther King's former lieutenant, Andrew Young. Ashe described him as 'a real leader of the African people'; and Young put him in the 'class of people who shape history'. Like Martin Luther King, he added, 'there are people with limited or no physical resources who fight injustice through the sheer force of their personalities . . . one of these days the SA Government may have to go to Sobukwe like the British went to Kenyatta'.

The movement towards a coalition of blacks and whites, built around a core of black unity, continued to attract support from leaders of the Coloured Labour Party, and from almost all the Homeland leaders. There was strong backing for Chief Kaiser Matanzima's call in October for 'a national convention of all races to discuss future policies and align them with the changing world.'[73]

The growing strength of Black Consciousness[74] had its predictable consequences on white South Africa; while the security froces continued to arrest militant black leaders (see below), some prominent figures in the Afrikaner Establishment re-evaluated the importance of what was happening. Prof. D. Kotze, Professor of Native Administration at the University of SA, warned that the Black Consciousness movement could not be countered merely by suppressing particular organizations. In an article in *Politikon*, a new journal of the Political Science Association of SA, he wrote that SA's 'white political system' needed to take serious note of the techniques, objectives and grievances of the Black Consciousness movement. 'It is not a movement that can be countered merely by suppressing specified organizations. It is the greatest single sustaining force behind the Black Consciousness movement. Ironically the SA official emphasis on colour distinction has undoubtedly encouraged the development of a colour exclusivism which is a fertile breeding ground for nationalism . . . Black Consciousness could prove disastrous in SA, and so could failure among whites to understand the reasons behind and the aspirations of this exclusiveness.'

BLACK POLITICAL MOVEMENTS
LABOUR PARTY AND FEDERAL PARTY
These two Coloured parties dominate the affairs of the Coloured Representative Council (CRC). The radical Labour Party, led by Sonny Leon, is committed to its destruction and willing to accept nothing less than full equality in the national Parliament. The Federal Party, led by Tom Swartz (who became ill and retired from politics at the end of 1974), is in favour of the CRC and is the favourite of the Government. But in 1974 defections from the FP turned it into a minority; the Labour Party was able to get a strong majority resolution passed which demanded the CRC's immediate dissolution; this produced a sharp confrontation with the Government (see Coloured Affairs below).

SA STUDENTS ORGANIZATION (Saso)
Although most of its top leadership was banned in 1973[75] Saso nevertheless found sufficient strength in 1974 to rally support on two occasions which brought them into conflict with the authorities. The first occasion was when they organized a rally with the Black People's Convention (BPC) in September to celebrate Frelimo's victory in Mozambique. Despite a ban imposed under the Riotous Assemblies Act, about 1,000 demonstrators appeared on the streets of Durban and Pietermaritzburg on 25 September. They were forcibly disbanded by the police who then arrested 19 of the remaining top Saso and BPC leaders, as well as members of the Black Workers' Allied Union. On 25 September, too, Saso organized a pro-Frelimo rally at the black University of the North (Turfloop). The police arrested the president of Saso at the university, Kaunda Sedibe, his predecessor, Jeremiah Nefolovhodowe, and another student leader, Cyril Rampaphosa. Thereupon virtually the entire student body of 1,400 marched to the local police station to demand their release. This confrontation plunged the troubled university back into a new round of confrontation between the authorities and the students which led the Government to appoint a commission of inquiry to determine the causes of the troubles. The September conflict had been preceded by another significant development in February after the former Turfloop

32

student and Saso leader, Abraham Tiro, had been killed by a time-bomb in Botswana.[76] The newly-formed Black Academic Staff Association at Turfloop issued a statement saying: 'We wish more power to Saso and to all those who identify themselves with the Tiros of our world. His death ... was not in vain . . . spectacular in its political significance (it) can only strengthen all those blacks in the country and anywhere on earth to mount up the struggle for truth and virtue.' Patrick Laurence, a well-informed writer, commented: 'The statement was highly significant: it meant black academics at the university had abandoned their previous neutrality and simultaneously come down on the side of black students.'[77]

BLACK PEOPLE'S CONVENTION (BPC)
With all except one of its top leaders banned or arrested in 1973[78] the BPC played only a minor role during 1974 except for its joint convenorship with Saso in the pro-Frelimo rally in Durban. Its offices in Johannesburg and King Williams Town were raided by the police after the rally and a number of its officials detained. Its new president is N. Farisani, a theological student.

BLACK RENAISSANCE CONVENTION (BRC)
The Black Renaissance Convention 'for Africans, Coloureds and Indians' was formed in 1974 and held its first meeting at Hammanskraal in December, from which all whites were barred on the grounds that their presence would inhibit free discussion and because of possible misreporting from the Press. Its sponsors, however, are the multi-racial SA Council of Churches, the Roman Catholic Church of SA and the Christian Institute, as well as the Association for Education and Cultural Advancement of Africans, Idamasa and the Dutch Reformed Church of Africa. Its organizing secretary, Father Smangaliso Mkhatshwa (see the African Mood above) said the BRC's purpose was to enable Africans, Coloureds and Indians to discuss their 'existential experience in SA'. While not primarily concerned with politics, political issues, he said, could obviously not be excluded; nor did it seek to exclude discussions with whites. But the first step, 'after the years of division among blacks forced on them by whites,' was for the different non-white groups to discover each other; once that was achieved 'something in the way of positive action' might emerge. A unanimous declaration accepted by the 320 delegates at the convention appealed for international boycott of the SA 'racist Government and racist institutions', including cultural, educational, economic, labour and military boycotts. It rejected Separate Development under the present apartheid system, and pledged support for a united and democratic SA.

EXILE MOVEMENTS
The African National Congress (ANC) and the Pan-Africanist Congress (PAC)[79] both continued to get official support from the OAU. A special committee of the OAU Liberation Committee was appointed to consider the future status of the African People's Democratic Union of SA (APDUSA) which has its exile headquarters in Lusaka. Both the ANC and the PAC were for the first time admitted as observers to the UN Political Committee. The ANC representative at the UN, Duma Nokwe, described SA as being 'ruled by an illegal regime which should be recognized as unlawful by the UN.'

BUTHELEZI'S REPORT-BACK MEETING IN SOWETO
The most direct challenge to the authorities came early in 1975 in a defiant speech from the KwaZulu leader, Chief Gatsha Buthelezi. On 9 February 1975, he addressed a mass meeting of Reef Africans in Soweto to report back on the eight-

hour talk held on 22 January 1975 with the Prime Minister. He began: 'We are all aware that the over-emphasis on our ethnic groupings, by the powers-that-be, was largely a matter of the old divide and rule technique, which is as old as the Roman Empire. That is why we as black leaders decided to meet at Umtata, on 8 November 1973. We knew that black people were one people, and their problems were the same, and had very little to do with ethnic grouping. We realized that we could only tackle these problems with any hope of any success at all if we have a common front and if we adopt a common strategy. With this end in view, we approached the Prime Minister to allow us to meet him together, so that we could present black grievances on a common platform. This the Prime Minister acceded to, and thus the interview he granted us on the 6 March last year. We presented the black man's case formally, and through memoranda we discussed with him. At the March 1974 meeting, we presented matters as follows:

1.(a) The meaning of independence; (b) The basic principles of land consolidation. 2. Racial discrimination. 3. The wage gap and disparity in revenue and expenditure in the Homelands. 4. The position of the urban blacks and the problems of black businessmen in urban areas. 5. The medium of instruction in African schools. 6. The phasing out of passes and influx control regulations. 7. The question of departments excluded from Homeland governments.

'All black leaders participated in the discussions. There was a strong divergence of opinion on most of the subjects discussed. The Prime Minister said we were free to ask for independence, and no one came forward among us to ask for what the Prime Minister calls "independence". The main reason being that most of the leaders could not accept the basis of such independence, purely on the basis of the 1936 Natives Land and Trust Act. Moreover, most of us felt it would not be right to do so, without a clear mandate from you. The Prime Minister stuck to his guns, that he would not contemplate going beyond the provisions of the 1936 Act, which means that blacks end up with nothing more than 13% of the whole area of SA, when they make 80% of the population. While we acknowledged the fact that the present Nationalist Government had bought more land for black occupation than any of the previous Governments, we could not accept that the mere purchase of all this land settles the question of land between black and white. There was no clarity on whether by "independence" the Prime Minister, on the one hand, and the black leaders, on the other, have in mind one and the same thing. The leaders spelled out point by point what they regarded as true independence. This area was never fully canvassed point by point in reply, except that the Prime Minister emphasized that he means independence in the dictionary sense of the word. Although there was a promise that during the current financial year, more money would be used (three times more than previously spent), the purchases under the 1936 Act can only be completed in five or ten years time. The main point here is that even if the full quota of land promised under the 1936 Act is purchased we still remain not fully consolidated into compact and contiguous "countries".

'On racial discrimination there was a very emotional and in-depth discussion on the basis that racial discrimination is an assault on the human dignity of blacks. The Prime Minister's view was that he would educate his own people, and that we should also educate our own people on attitudes. The Prime Minister said that racial friction could not be avoided through legislation, but by education. He admitted that there were some among his own people who addressed blacks in a crude manner. He said the other side of the coin was that there were certain blacks who were arrogant when they met whites.

'On the point that there was the wage gap and disparity in the revenue and expenditure of these so-called Homelands and the revenue and expenditure for whites, it was decided to set up a committee of experts, one nominated by blacks, and one by the Prime Minister. They were to go into the whole contention by black leaders, that Africans in general, and the Homelands Governments in particular, are not getting a fair share of services from taxes paid directly and indirectly by Africans. Black leaders requested the Government to devise ways and means of closing the gap in salaries paid to different racial groups.

'On the medium of instruction, that the language used in schools in the so-called "white areas" should be the same with that used in the Homelands, the Prime Minister suggested that the Minister of Bantu Administration goes into the legal constitutional and educational aspects and then report at the next meeting.

'On urban blacks, and black businessmen in urban areas, the Prime Minister suggested a full day to be set aside to discuss the problems of urban blacks, as the Prime Minister admitted that the subject was important and big enough to warrant the setting aside of the whole day to discuss it. That is how the Conference we had with the Prime Minister on the 22 January 1975 came about.

'When we approached the Prime Minister initially, we did so in order to discuss black problems, regardless of whether they were rural or urban, as black oppression in SA is the same. It is something based on colour and it is a system which forces all blacks, wherever they are, to live under the most untenable conditions, under which no other racial group, even those who share discrimination with Africans, has to live.'

Buthelezi then criticized those who questioned the credentials of the rural leaders to speak for urban Africans. 'The struggle of the black man is one,' he said.

Buthelezi reviewed in detail the discussions on black urban problems such as influx control regulations, the place of black professionals, civic rights, public transport, mass population removals, ethnic grouping, education and black trade union rights, and continued: *The Detente in Southern Africa*: This discussion was led by me, and was probably the most controversial part of our whole conference with the PM. I was supported by the Chief Minister of BophuthaTswana. Other leaders who participated in this particular discussion were the Chief Ministers of the Transkei, Lebowa, Gazankulu and the Ciskei.

'In my presentation, I congratulated and applauded the PM and the President of Zambia on their efforts to promote detente in southern Africa. I also read excerpts from a letter from a PAC refugee abroad, in which he praised the PM and expressed hopes that the PM would rise to the occasion, and that his new deal would not just be 'a repetition of the same policies that are already unacceptable to the international community at large'. This African patriot expressed a hope that 'the PM can certainly deliver a lightning stroke from the southern Africa dark horizon and save our people and country, as a nation, from being the international community's "whipping boy" that should be pilloried at every other following conference. I quoted other excerpts, but I will only end up with that one to show you to what extent I felt I should encourage the PM on black expectations, after he had taken initiatives on a detente in southern Africa.

'I reminded the PM of what he had said to us in March 1974 that he does not believe in racial discrimination but in differentiation, and I told him that we can hardly tell the difference between the two. I reminded him that, by co-operating with his Government in implementing this policy, we had been slated as "collaborators with the oppressors", by certain elements within SA and others outside SA. I reminded him that there were those among us who do not believe in apartheid as a philosophy, but who have co-operated merely because there were no other alternatives allowed in the interests of a peaceful settlement being found. I pointed out the hopes raised that blacks were going to have a meaningful change in view of his "give-us-six-months", speech.

'I told the PM that this was to us a natural corollary of his initiatives in the present detente in southern Africa. We hoped to share power, and decision-making, in a new and meaningful way. I told the PM of the assurances I was given by President Kaunda when I visited him in December 1973 that he also believes in a peaceful change on the basis of the Lusaka Manifesto. I reminded the PM that we had presented the Lusaka Manifesto to him in March 1974 as a reasonable basis for a peaceful change in SA. I told the PM that President Kaunda had then told me that he believed in a meaningful dialogue with SA, but that a meaningful dialogue should take place between us within SA first before he was interested in it. I told the PM of a similar statement by the President of Liberia to me this year, when he said that if the PM wanted to meet him as an equal, that he would be interested only if the PM regarded his black brothers in SA as equals first.

'I told the PM that I had told the President of Liberia that, although the PM does meet us as equals around the table, as today, it was too early for me to judge whether we are moving towards real and meaningful equality in SA. I told the PM that President Tolbert had expressed the view that they would be guided by us, their black brothers, as to what stance they should adopt towards SA.

'I told the PM that we do not regard the present Government policy on consolidating these areas, on the basis of the 1936 Natives Land Act, as leading us to such real and meaningful equality; but that after his Senate speech, his Nigel speech, and Mr. R. F. Botha's speech at the UN, in which the latter condemned racial discrimination, we were full of expectations, and that our hopes had been raised even on a more meaningful consolidation of the Homeland areas; and that I hoped that he would seriously consider a federal formula on the basis of properly consolidated Homeland areas.

'I then stated that although the item on detente had been placed on the agenda with the concurrence of my fellow black leaders I wanted to point out that I did not want to embarrass them by assuming that they also agree with me on the part of my memorandum I was then about to read. I told the PM that I took full responsibility for this part of my memorandum. I warned: We have been prepared to endure abuse in the hope that the Government's policy may be a road to real fulfilment for blacks. If this road, as appears under the circumstances described above, is leading only to a cul-de-sac, then our only alternative is to seek fulfilment not in unreal "separate freedoms", but in one SA and in the only seat of power which is Parliament. I went on: 'I would like to make it crystal clear that I am not saying these things in any spirit of illwill or threats, but I fell that it is my moral duty, at this point in time, to point out the only logical alternatives we have, if we do not want our people to resort to civil disobedience and disruption of services in this land. Not that I intend leading my people in this direction at the moment, but I do feel, judging by the mood of my people, that it is timely that I should point out that if no meaningful change is forthcoming for them through the Government's policies this will come as a logical alternative. I believe in avoiding situations when we, as South Africans, can only hurt each other, with no real victors on either side. At the same time, I want to say that I cannot be expected to successfully ward off the venting of pent-up frustrations of my people, if the Government continually fails to offer them anything meaningful through their policy.'

Buthelezi then quoted a number of excerpts from Mr R. F. Botha's speech at the United Nations. Extracts will be found in the essay on *Southern Africa: the Secret Diplomacy of Detente* in this volume.

'I quoted some of these extracts to show the PM what has heightened black expectations as a result of his utterances, and the utterances of SA's Permanent Representative at the UN.

'The Hon. Chief L. M. Mangope referred to the March 1974 Conference and the PM's statement that he did not believe in racial discrimination. He asked whether we are going to be separate and equal, and wanted to know what the import of the PM's speeches was, and that of Mr R. F. Botha at the UN. He wanted to know what had been done to educate the people in SA to avoid harmful racial incidents. Prof. H. W. Ntsanwisi praised the PM for his role in promoting detente and hoped that this would lead to an improvement of conditions for black people in SA. The Hon. Paramount-Chief K. D. Matanzima supported him, and also pleaded with the PM to take the black leaders into his confidence on the question of where SA was going. Dr C. N. Phatudi also stressed the expectancy created by the recent speeches. Mr L. L. Sebe expressed hopes of meaningful change and the expectancy he had encountered in his travels, even abroad.

'The PM repeated the main theme of his speech in the Senate, dealing with peace and co-operation in southern Africa. He outlined the reactions in Zambia and elsewhere and then dealt in detail with his speech in Nigel. Quoting from the typewritten text of the speech, the PM said that he had not asked for six-months for himself, or for his party, or for his policy, but for SA, and that even those who refused to give him that time will see where SA stands in 6-12 months. He was referring here not to the domestic affairs of SA but to the question of SA's position in Africa and the world. He repeated that if peace could be achieved in southern Africa, the black leaders would appreciate where SA whould then stand. The PM said that those people who now feted the Homeland leaders at conferences had had their opportunity in the past and asked what they had done for the black people, and leaders of that period. The black leaders were now recognized as such and could discuss matters with him as equals. He said that Government policy was indeed to get away from purely racial discrimination. However, he pointed out that there are many differences which existed in SA's multi-national composition. He said that very day's meeting with black leaders on matters of vital importance to them was proof of how the Government was trying to eliminate friction and how the black leaders shared in the considerations, and decisions on matters affecting black people.

'On the question of sharing power in one Parliament, the PM said that this was not the policy of his party and his Government. However, black leaders would eventually have sole power in independent States. Meanwhile, more and more opportunities would be created for black people to exercise power and responsibilities in the "Homelands", and to obtain experience in, for example, international affairs. The PM mentioned in this connection the recent—what he called—"multi-national" delegation to the UN and the training of black diplomats and Information Officers abroad.

'Referring to my memorandum in which, as you have heard, I referred to civil disobedience and disruption of services if black aspirations are not met, the PM said that I should consider my position and statements. He said no one would be allowed to take the law into his hands, and SA would be administered on the basis of law and order.

'He said he envisaged independence for all Homelands and promised that SA would, after their independence, provide financial and technical expertise to the new countries. He said that we must wait and see what happens when the Transkei gets its independence.

'*The question of amnesty for SA political exiles and prisoners*: This discussion was led by me, and most leaders participated with great feeling in it. When the PM asked me what I meant by political prisoners. I said I have in mind people like Mr Nelson Mandela. I told the PM that even on the basis of common law offenders, a remission of sentence is given after a certain period of time, and I appealed that this matter be dealt with in the same way. I pointed out that the Rhodesian political detainees had been released as a result of the PM's initiatives. I felt this was the psychological moment to release our own political detainees. The Chief Minister of the Transkei, in supporting my presentation, said that special consideration ought to be given to those who left the country without a passport, and who now wished to return to 'Homelands' such as the Transkei. The PM said that if people left SA and did not commit a crime, and were not communists, but that their only crime was leaving the country without a passport, he would consider their return sympathetically, if the leaders vouch for them. The same applied to those who left with an exit permit. The PM said that he had warned these people at the time that if they had been sentenced by a court for breaking the law and later fled the country, they would receive no mercy. Referring to one of the prisoners whose names had been mentioned, and others who are in prison with him, the PM said the prisoner in question boasted of being a communist in court, and he had not changed his mind. He said the same applied to some of his fellow-prisoners. He went on to say that all people in SA, blacks and whites, needed protection against the aspirations of communists such as the individual who did not, in his opinion, speak for black people, but on behalf of the Communist Party. (This was obviously a reference to Bram Fischer.)

'On the questions put to the PM by Dr Phatudi and others and by me on Mr Robert Sobukwe, the PM said that Mr Sobukwe did not fall into the above-mentioned category. In other words, he was not a communist, even though he had other problems. He said that his case was reviewed from time to time. On being asked by me on whether he could not initiate a special review of Mr Sobukwe's case, at his special instance, the PM said he would do so, although he could not bind the Minister of Justice and vice-versa.

'Other issues discussed were Foreign Investments in "the Homelands", the powers and functions of Commissioners-General and the proposed new autonomous Homeland Development Corporations. I will not go into them.

'I have come here because I believe that I have a moral obligation to report to you as our constituents. I do not consider that it is good enough for me to trust that you will get tit-bits of what was discussed through mass media. That is why I am here to day. As you have seen on peripheral issues, there were a few concessions, here and there. I believe that it is time we hear from you whether we can adopt a new strategy in the light of the reactions to our presentation of your grievances by the PM. At the same time, since I went so far as to issue the warning of what might happen, I felt that I need to come and explain exactly what I said, and exactly what I meant. I have not deviated from my path of non-violence, in spite of all the violence arrayed against us, as the powerless and voiceless people of this land. Since our people can never meet violence with violence, even if one assumed some wanted this, I do believe that they have other non-violent methods which will come to hand automatically if nothing meaningful emerges for them in terms of sharing real decision-making, political power and of sharing the wealth of SA which we have also worked to produce, over decades. These are not threats at all, but responsible warnings of what is logical, if the detente leaves us out in the cold in this part of southern Africa, with nothing meaningful for us in terms of the sharing of wealth and decision-making I have referred to above.

'All these things cannot be over-simplified. These things mean an uphill struggle such as the Afrikaner himself had. In many ways our struggle is, and will be, much more arduous than that of the Afrikaner. The Afrikaner at least had the advantage of a white skin, the veritable measuring-rod of security, and privilege in SA for the last 300 years. What I have come to say is that we need to think seriously of the only alternatives that might be forced on us by circumstances: white intransigence and white greed. I fear that if we are taken by surprise and we are caught napping, I would never forgive myself for not issuing these warnings. These are not things I say lightly, nor are these things we can be jubilant about. These spell for us the painful path which all oppressed people have at one time or another to traverse as there are hardly any short-cuts to freedom.

'Our Afrikaner countrymen, who are today wielding power over us, should know these things better than anyone since their own memories of their own subjugation are still so fresh, being less than a century ago. I realize only too well that, just like the Afrikaner, our path to freedom is full of dangers. The Afrikaner will bear me out that this is a path fraught with suffering, and I am afraid even with death, for some of us. The consolation I have, which I hope is well founded, is that the Afrikaner himself did not ascend to power only through bloodshed. My daily prayer for him is that God should give him the grace He gave the English to bow to the inevitable while there is time.

'Most of you might expect miracles from us. Some of you use us even to ventilate frustrations, as if we retard the pace of your march to freedom. That is one of the reasons why I have decided to come and tell it to you, like it is! This I am doing in the hope that you will realize that we have a great moral duty to make sacrifices for our posterity. The Afrikaner who is ruling us today is reaping the fruits of many sacrifices his forebears made for him. The way to freedom was sprinkled for him with sweat, with blood and with tears. If we expected any less than this, it can only mean one thing—we are living in a Fool's Paradise.

'We, as your leaders, cannot dictate sacrifices to you. We must liaise with you, and reach some consensus as to where we are going, and how we are getting there. We have to learn from past experiences and avoid some of the mistakes of some of our predecessors. It is no longer good enough to promote sporadic, dramatic actions, which will be topical in the World Press for a few weeks or even months, and then peter out. We must aim for something which will make our rulers come to terms with us not just on the basis of a make-shift arrangement, but on the basis of finding a formula for peaceful co-existence of the people of SA of every race, and of every colour. It is no longer good enough to blast us for not "talking sense into the Prime Minister"—as some of you would say. We want to know alternative suggestions given direct to us and not through mass media. This we must do, if we are all convinced that black solidarity is the answer to black oppression. We do not pretend to be some demi-Gods; we are human like each one of you; we are no more devils or angels than anyone of you can be either of those things. We have power and we can use it effectively, only if we do not stop by talking black solidarity, but if we act as if we really believe in it.'

HOMELAND LEADERSHIP

A major division of opinion recurred among the nine Homeland leaders in 1974 when the Transkei's Chief Minister, Kaiser Matanzima, revoked on the 1973 Black Summit decisions taken at Umtata which agreed on a confederation of the black Homelands as one of the prerequisites for independence.[80] He put a resolution through the Transkei Assembly calling for independence within five years. Chief Gatsha Buthelezi expressed regret that the solidarity of Homelands' leaders had been broken; but Lebowa's Minister of Interior, Collins Ramusi, spoke more strongly, calling Matanzima's decision 'a betrayal'. An effort to repair the damage was partially successful when Matanzima agreed with six of his Homelands' colleagues to affirm their belief that federation offers a possible alternative for the future (see the Federal Issue above).

Despite this breach, all except two of the Homeland leaders continued to work closely together on all issues other than separate independence for the Homelands. The two outsiders are Chief Wessels Motha of Basotho Qwaqwa and Chief Patrick Mphephu of Venda. The former clings to an isolated position—at one time it was thought he might wish to join up with his neighbour Lesotho, but even this possibility he ruled out in 1974 on the ground of the 'instability' of Lesotho. Mphephu, a conservative traditionalist, concentrates mostly on defending his minority position within his own authority. Another Homeland leader who has found himself fighting hard to maintain his power base is Chief Lucas Mangope of BophuthaTswana. He, however, continued his sharply critical attutude towards the Government. The strongest core within the Homeland leadership is formed by Buthelezi, Chief Pathudi of Lebowa and Prof. Ntsanwisi of Gazankulu. This trio agrees over most issues and sets the pace for the rest, with Buthelezi as the vanguard leader.

During 1974 the simmering argument about the role of Homeland leaders as spokesmen for urban Africans burst into the open when the question of negotiating with the Prime Minister over the conditions of the urban dwellers assumed greater importance. The editor of *The World* (a black newspaper), Percy Qoboza, wrote that black urban rejection of the Homelands did not mean they did not accept the leadership of people such as Chiefs Buthelezi and Matanzima. But the leader of the National Convention of Urban Africans, E. L. Manyosi, rejected the right of Homeland leaders to speak for urban blacks: 'We refuse to be led by countryside leaders, because they know very little about what really affects us in the cities.' Buthelezi replied: 'We, as Homeland leaders, feel troubled about the lack of security of our urban blacks. We think if there is a dangerous flashpoint in the future as far as race relations are concerned, it will be provided by this disregard for the rights of urban Africans. Homeland leaders have always articulated what they know to be the wishes and aspirations of blacks, including urban blacks. We have no qualms of conscience about this because we have done the best we can in the circumstances within which we are operating.'

HOMELANDS : INTERNAL AFFAIRS IN 1974

(See map on p. B488.)

BASOTHO QWAQWA

This Homeland[81] became self-governing under the name of Qwaqwa on 1 November 1974. It covers c. 61,000 ha of mountainous country on the edge of the Drakensberg along the Lesotho border. Its capital, Phuthadithjaba, is planned to have a population of c. 40,000; the present population of the whole territory is only 145,000 although it is supposed to represent more than 1m South Sothos. The territory's Chief Executive Councillor is Chief Wessels Motha. Unlike other Homelands, the Legislative Assembly is not packed with chiefs, the majority of its members being commoners. (Chief Motha was defeated in an election in 1975.)

Chief Motha called on Sotho-speaking chiefs and tribesmen living in the Transkei and Ciskei to throw in their lot with Qwaqwa. There is a possibility of Qwaqwa opting for full union with independent Lesotho. Quaqwa was reported[82] in October to have become a 'dumping ground' for c. 2,000 workless and homeless families. They were brought by truck to Tseki at Witzieshoek, where there were no amenities; most were taken from the Thaba'Nchu area of BophuthaTswana, where they were ordered to leave by the regional authority.

BANTU HOMELANDS

Name of Homeland	Name of People	Population[1]	Constitutional Development[2]	Capital	Head of Authority
Transkei	Xhosa	1,734,000 (3,005,000)	Chap. 2 (1963)	Umtata	Kaiser Matanzima
Ciskei	Xhosa	524,000 (924,000)	Chap. 2 (Aug 1972)	Zwelitsha	Lennox L. Sebe
KwaZulu	Zulu	2,097,000 (4,026,000)	Chap. 1 (Apr 1972)	Nongoma	Gatsha Buthelezi
BophuthaTswana	Tswana	884,000 (1,658,000)	Chap. 2 (June 1972)	Heystekrand	Lucas Mangope
Lebowa	N. Sotho (Pedi)	1,083,000 (2,019,000)	Chap. 2 (Sept 1972)	Lebowakgomo	Cedric Phatudi
Gazankulu	Shangaan and Tsonga	267,000 (649,000)	Chap. 2 (Feb 1973)	Giyani	Prof. Hudson Ntsanwisi
Venda	Venda	264,000 (358,000)	Chap. 2 (Feb 1973)	Sibasa	Patrick Mphephu
Basotho Qwaqwa	S. Sotho	24,000 (1,254,000)	Chap. 2 (Nov 1974)	Phuthadithjaba	Chief Wessels Motha
—	Swazi	118,000	—	—	—
—	S. Ndebele	(233,021)	—	—	—
—	N. Ndebele	(181,748)	—	—	—

[1] The first number is the resident population; the total population is given in brackets. Taken from 1969 figures in *Horrel*: African Reserves.
[2] Chap. 1 provides for a Legislative Assembly and Executive Council with its own revenue fund but limited powers, closely supervised. Laws may not be inconsistent with Acts of Parliament. Chap. 2 provides for a Legislative Assembly and Executive Council with its own revenue fund The stages of development were laid down in the Bantu Homelands Constitution Act (1971).

Source: *Horrell: Institute of Race Relations Survey, 1972, Johannesburg.*

BOPHUTHATSWANA[83]

A crisis developed in the ruling party (BNP) during 1974 after a group had introduced a vote of no confidence in the BNP leader and Chief Minister, Lucas Mangope, and called for his resignation. Mangope was accused of interfering in the affairs of the Madikwe regional authority; of writing to the Commissioner-General asking for the removal from the Cabinet of Chief Herman Maseloane (Minister of Works and deputy-leader of the BNP) without consulting his Cabinet colleagues; and of establishing a Development Fund in his own private capacity. Mangope thereupon asked the Government to dismiss both Chief Maseloane and Chief James Toto (Minister of Agriculture) from his Cabinet. Although a BNP meeting voted in April to expel the two men, Maseloane and Toto petitioned the Supreme Court which granted an interdict calling on Mangope to show why the men should not be reinstated. On 9 September Mangope reinstated them.

41

The SA Government has persisted in its refusal to allow Mangope to dismiss the rebel Ministers in his Cabinet. In a bid to resolve the stalemate within the BNP Mangope resigned from the party in November and formed his own Democratic Party. Mangope later claimed that the Ministers of Education and Justice, 41 MPs and leading chiefs had joined his new party.

During the crisis Mangope, like Buthelezi, accused the SA Government of plotting against him by mounting a 'campaign of political interference and intrigue' to oust him from power. He said that the Government took exception 'to anyone who has any independence of mind. They do not like some of the criticisms I have levelled against their policies and their implementation.' He particularly attacked the role of Commissioners-General: 'If they are supposed to be amabassadors they should behave as such, not as our bosses and rulers. Their jobs should be streamlined or else done away with.' Mangope, however, welcomed the Prime Minister's proposals for changes in Homelands' financing, announced in October. These provided for Homelands to receive a share of taxes levied on goods consumed in the Homeland area as well as a share of taxes paid by companies operating there, and that the Homelands would decide how industry would develop instead of having decisions made for them by semi-Government bodies.

A capital town for BophuthaTswana was being built at Heystekrand, north of Rustenburg.

CISKEI[84]

A number of white-controlled towns were released to the Ciskei in 1974, including Frankfort, Keiskammahoek, Lady Frere, Peddie and a portion of Braunschweig. The resettlement township of Dimbaza[85] was declared an 'industrial growth point' where special concessions would be available to private entrepreneurs. The Chief Minister, Lennox Sebe, said that the Dimbaza area had already attracted industry and his policy was to correct 'any mistakes made in the past'. Infrastructure was being provided and the township was getting a new railway line.

Negotiations have continued to merge the Ciskei with its neighbour, the Transkei. While Chief Sebe said amalgamation was inevitable in the future he did not favour it at this stage.

GAZANKULU[86]

Opening the Gazankulu Legislative Assembly in Giyani in March, the Chief Minister, Prof. Hudson Ntsanwisi, appealed to white SA to give the Shangaan-Tsonga people 'a stake in the economy of the country so that we have something to defend'. He said that good relations would only come about if there was a fair consolidation of Gazankulu and if there were meaningful dialogue between the races in which 'paternalism is relegated to the limbo of the past'. Later, Ntsanwisi stressed that Gazankulu was far from being a viable territory. Its financial dependence on 'handouts from the Republican Government make a mockery of the concept of self-development and independence of our people'. Any Homeland that aimed at being economically viable should be able to provide employment for the majority of its people; yet in Gazankulu there was 'a complete lack of employment opportunities'. As a result, most of its population was domiciled outside the territory.

Negotiations have started for the merging of Gazankulu with its neighbour, Lebowa.

KWAZULU[87]

KwaZulu continued its existence as being only in the first stage of Homeland development which means that it has even fewer powers than the tiniest of the

Homelands. Although the Legislative Assembly voted in May to ask the SA Government to allow it to move towards the second phase of the constitutional programme, progress was delayed because of a controversy over the date for its first elections. The Assembly insists that Zulus should apply for citizenship cards and use them instead of the SA 'reference books' (passes) as proof of identity when voting in the elections. However, people were slow in applying for their cards; according to Chief Gatsha Buthelezi, Zulus in white-controlled areas fear that they would lose rights of residence in those areas if they held Zulu citizenship cards.

Buthelezi continued to accuse the Republican Government and BOSS of plotting to get rid of him.[88] He alleged in May that Francois Fouche of BOSS had been instrumental in founding and financing the opposition *Umkhonto wa Shaka* (Shaka's Spear). A motion was passed in the Assembly requesting the SA Government to empower KwaZulu to control or forbid the formation of political parties in the territory until after independence.

The Bantu Administration Minister, M. C. Botha, turned down the KwaZulu request for limited self-government because, he alleged, Buthelezi had denied his own countrymen the opportunity of exercising their political rights in a general election and was opposed to a multi-party system in KwaZulu. Botha also said that a self-governing territory had to have clearly defined boundaries, and KwaZulu would only have these when the new districts in Natal had been promulgated.

The Executive Councillor for Community Affairs, Barney Dladla,[89] was at the centre of a dispute over the right of Councillors to act without consulting the Cabinet. He had acted as an intermediary between certain strikers in Durban and their employers. Dladla was moved to the Justice Department, but in a further clash with the Assembly he was removed from office by 78 votes to nil.

Faction fighting in the Msinga district persisted in 1974 despite arrests and detentions. There was also feuding in Soweto and KwaZulu between tribesmen of the Nkandla and Kranskop districts. At least 20 were reported killed.

Buthelezi continued to demand control of the Zululand coastline and territorial waters. He said in March that even if the Republic gave KwaZulu all the land promised under the 1936 Land and Trust Act, the land would not be adequate to make KwaZulu a country which could stand on its own.

In November Vorster wrote to Buthelezi rebuking him for speaking out on issues of self-government and for interference in other Homelands' affairs by addressing meetings there without obtaining prior authority from the local leaders.

KwaZulu's new capital is being built at Ulundi.

Buthelezi offered a Cabinet post to Robert Sobukwe, the former PAC leader, still under restriction at the end of 1974.

LEBOWA[90]

The Government of the Lebowa Homeland (formerly North Sotho) laid claim in 1974 to a huge tract of territory comprising one-third of the Transvaal, including part of Gazankulu and BophuthaTswana and several major 'white' towns, including Pietersburg, Potgietersrust, Lydenburg, Nelspruit and Witbank, as well as white farms, mines, and the southern half of the Kruger National Park. This claim, drawn up by its radical Interior Minister, Collins Ramusi, was its own Land Committee's answer to the Pretoria Government's consolidation plan. Against the SA Government's readiness to concede 8,000 sq. miles as belonging to Lebowa under the 1936 Land Act, the Homeland Government was demanding no less than 29,000 sq. miles covering the whole of central Transvaal between Botswana and Mozambique. The Lebowa Committee's report said that all whites and non-Sotho blacks who wished to live within the Homeland would be welcomed. The Legislative Assembly later passed a resolution asking its Cabinet to draft a Bill entrenching the rights of whites, Coloureds and Indians in the territory.

Lebowa leaders met the Prime Minister and the Minister of Bantu Affairs on 7 May to discuss the land claims. The Lebowa's Chief Minister, Dr Cedric Phatudi, said there was a need for an amalgamation or federation of Homelands to control areas where people of various ethnic origins are intermingled—a particularly complex problem in Lebowa's case. Opposition to Lebowa's claims was expressed by BophuthaTswana, Ndebele and, at first, by Gazankulu; but talks between Lebowa and Gazankulu on a united Homeland for their respective peoples were resumed in January 1975.

Phatudi joined Buthelezi and Mangope in protesting against SA Government interference in internal Homeland affairs. In November he accused the SA Commissioner-General, Gert Bezuidenhout, of addressing a meeting in the Moutse region—when land consolidation and removal of the Moutse people were discussed—'without our knowledge'. He told a public meeting that he had warned the Commissioner-General at a Cabinet meeting 'that he has no right to meddle in Lebowa politics'. The Moutse region has an estimated population of 29,000 who must vacate the area and move to Emmerpan in order to make way for an influx of South Ndebele, as ordered by the SA Government under its land consolidation proposals.

In March 1974 the leader of the Lebowa opposition National Party, Chief Matlala,[91] voluntarily dissolved the party and joined Dr Phatudi's ruling Lebowa People's Party.

Lebowa's designated new capital of Lebowakgomo was still only an empty site in 1974, with half-finished buildings and no population. Reporters wrote that members of the Lebowa Government were 'not ecstatic about moving 30 km out of Pietersburg into the bush, even though they will live in smart new houses'.

NDEBELE

Many Ndebele live in Lebowa. Others live in parts of BophuthaTswana. Four Ndebele tribal authorities exist, one having the status of a regional authority, but they fall under either the Lebowa or BophuthaTswana governments. Some chiefs continued their campaign for a Homeland of their own and opposed Lebowa's proposals to incorporate all the Ndebele.

SWAZI[92]

The SA Government revealed in the Assembly that c. 59,800 Swazis living in the Legogote-Nsikazi area (east of White River and Nelspruit) would have to move after compulsory land had been acquired. This land would then cease to be a black area. They would be resettled along the Swazi border on less fertile land. The chiefs concerned sent letters to the Commissioner-General and Mrs Helen Suzman MP expressing their strong opposition. Mrs Suzman described the Government's plan as 'just another of their unsympathetic inhuman ideological exercises'.

TRANSKEI[93]

In March 1974 Chief Minister Matanzima moved in the territory's Legislative Assembly that the Republican Government would be asked to grant full independence to the Transkei within five years. He stipulated that during this period the remainder of the land due to the Transkei under the 1936 Trust and Land Act should be added, but that such a grant of land should not prejudice the Transkei's claims to additional districts (Port St Johns, Elliot and Maclear, East Griqualand, etc.). In September the Government said it was in favour of granting independence to the Transkei. A committee of experts would deal with the necessary preparatory work, examining the legal, constitutional, financial, administrative and other questions. The question of the possible amalgamation of Transkei and Ciskei was a matter which rested in the hands of the two Homeland Governments concerned.

The opposition Transkei Democratic Party (TDP) condemned Matanzima's plan and warned that it could result in economic disaster. A TDP leader described independence at a time when Transkei's unemployment figure was estimated at half a million as 'the second national suicide of the Xhosa people in SA's history'.

Matanzima threatened[94] to jail TDP members after independence if they continued to call for revolutionary change. He branded one TDP group as 'revolutionary fellow-travellers of Peking and Moscow', and called on the Opposition leader, Knowledge Guzana, to throw out these 'rotten eggs'. Transkei lost two prominent politicians in 1974. The senior paramount chief, Victor Poto of Western Pondoland, died in April. He had been leader of the TDP when it was dominant in Transkei politics before the SA Government intervened on Matanzima's side. The other was of Curnick Ndamse, who also died in April. He had left Matanzima's party in 1973 after a series of publicized differences of opinion and entered the Legislative Assembly as an independent.[95]

The Transkei's budget for the 1974-75 financial year was a record R70 m, an increase of R14 m over 1973-74, Education took the biggest slice, with an estimated expenditure of R17 m.

VENDA

The traditionalist Chief Minister of Venda, Chief Patrick Mphephu, who had been defeated in the 1973 elections by the Venda Independence Party (VIP) but had secured enought support from chiefs to give him a majority in the Legislative Assembly,[96] launched his own political party in 1974, the Venda National Party (VNP). (Earlier he had threatened to ban all political activity in his territory.) He said his party would be tradition-oriented and concerned with preserving the powers and functions of the chiefs. It would aim at independence, but would not negotiate for this on the basis of the existing land consolidation plans.

When the Legislative Assembly began its session in March some of Mphephu's former supporters began to cross the floor to join the Opposition until the chief's majority had dropped from 24 to only six. After only 11 days Mphephu announced the Assembly's closure. The VIP leader, Baldwin Mudau, said he was confident of being able to exercise a *coup de grace* when the Assembly opened again 'provided there is no interference from European officials'. Mudau's vision of the future is in line with the majority of Homeland leaders. 'We can never have an independent Venda by itself. Whoever thinks that is dreaming.' He accused Mphephu of being an isolationist. Referring to the 'terrorist threat' to SA, Mudau said[97] that Venda (which borders the Limpopo River) would be the first battleground 'but if we are to defend the country we should have something to defend'. Immediate reforms were necessary if the Venda were to play a proper role in defending the country, including freedom to own land throughout SA, equality of job opportunity, equal pay for equal work, and relaxation of pass laws. Another prerequisite was for Pretoria to end its 'interference' in Venda politics.

THE HOMELANDS' ECONOMIC AND SOCIAL CONDITIONS

The first detailed study of living conditions and attitudes of the Homelands' people was conducted in 1974 by two SA companies, Markinor and Quadrant International SA.[98] It covered the four largest Homelands, comprising 83% of the Homelands' population: Transkei, KwaZulu, Lebowa and BophuthaTswana. The average per capita income of Homeland people was R7 a month, compared with a white SA per capita income of R127 a month. In the Homelands 25% of the households earn no income at all. The inflation rate was running at 14% from September 1973 to September 1974, while over the same period in 'white' SA, inflation was running at 8%. White Homelands' incomes showed some improvements. These were not sufficient to keep pace with inflation. A crucial problem facing the Homelands is that 50% of their population is under the age of 15, while in 'white' SA only 31% is under 15. There are also twice as many women as men. Thus every second woman lives on her own with no means of support. The survey found a severe lack of jobs, lack of recreation facilities, poor transportation, and inadequate schools and shops. Nevertheless, 58% of Homeland people interviewed were in favour of the Homelands' concept. They said the major attraction was the absence of whites. To be free of whites meant to be free of police raids, free of passes and to have the opportunity to run a business, own a house, buy land or raise cattle. Those who rejected the Homeland idea (20% of those interviewed) were critical of the way they were run. They complained of no real freedom, that one still needed permits, that everything was run on ethnic grounds, and that there was no free interchange. Their feeling was still that whites were omnipresent. 32% were dissatisfied with their Governments, especially in KwaZulu and BophuthaTswana (those with the largest urban areas). Homeland Governments were blamed for the lack of progress, the exclusiveness and selfishness of their officials, the lack of real independence from the white power structure and their own territorial Government's failure to consult the people before reaching decisions affecting the Homelands.

The SA Government's plans to develop the Homelands to achieve some semblance of self-sufficiency and nationhood came under attack from the most surprising quarter of all in 1974, the man who originally formulated the entire Homelands blueprint on behalf of the Government in 1950, Professor Frederick Tomlinson. He criticized[99] the Government for not having accepted in 1954 his Commission's proposals that white capital should be used to start diversified economies in the Homelands. 'Because of the pressure of circumstances the Government has supported secondary development since 1970. Our view in this respect was correct, but SA has lost 15 valuable years,' he said. He also criticized the Government for not consolidating the Homelands as a priority and for not appointing a board to advise on all aspects of Homeland development. He went on: 'At the time the report appeared there was the opportunity to fire great idealism, enthusiasm and support by starting large-scale and ambitious programmes which gripped the imagination and in which the whole population co-operated. Instead we got important but fragmentary and only relatively small-scale efforts up to 1970 . . . White SA should be careful that future generations do not reproach it one day.'

Meanwhile, the Government's efforts to attract capital investment continued. It was announced in December that a development corporation would be set up for each Homeland in 1975. These would be established 'in accordance with the Government's policy to involve the African people in increasing measure in the development of their Homelands,' according to the Bantu Administration Minister. The corporations would be authorized to grant housing loans, loans for commercial undertakings, the erection of commercial buildings and the financing of farmers and co-operative undertakings. Each corporation would be controlled and managed by a board of 10 directors, of whom four would be nominated by the Homeland Government concerned. These corporations would take over the functions of the regional administrations of the Bantu Investment Corporation (BIC). It was also announced that the Xhosa Development Corporation (XDC)—for Transkei and Ciskei—would soon have at least two blacks on its board. The Chief Minister of the

Ciskei, Lennox Sebe, welcomed the move, as in the past the XDC had 'suffered in African eyes from being seen as a white organization making decisions on behalf of blacks'. By mid-1974 the BIC could claim to have attracted twelve foreign investors to the Homelands, with investments totalling R7.25 m, and to have made total capital investments of R65 m since 1959. But its performance was already far behind the targets it had set itself, let alone the required level of new jobs necessary to relieve the desperate unemployment situation in the Homelands. Its managing director admitted[100] that the BIC had created only 13,500 industrial jobs in four years, whereas the annual number of required new industrial jobs was at least 20,000.

The BIC was strongly criticized by the Tswana leader, Chief Mangope, for being 'a vast bureaucracy which smothers African enterprise with red tape', and for failing to consult sufficiently with Homeland governments. It was also the target of allegations of fraud and corruption. (See Corruption above.) Up to the end of 1974 BIC still had no African directors or staff. It engaged in a vigorous advertising campaign abroad, especially in the UK under the names of Homeland leaders. Chief Matanzima was quoted as saying: 'SA has the most stable Government on the African continent. And it is a capitalistic Government dedicated to free enterprise . . . I offer you an investment in one of SA's nine black Homelands.' Lebowa's Chief Minister, Cedric Phatudi, pointed out the advantage of low wages as an incentive to investors, and the lack of 'militant trade unions'; 'in short the black proletariat in the black Homelands is ready, willing and able to do a decent day's work for a fair salary. How does that compare with the situation in your country?' The BIC managing director, Dr Johannes Adendorff, was displeased by a British proposal to invest R3.2 m annually in the Homelands (submitted to the Conservative Party's Bow Group by an investment analyst) because he suspected that the proposal contained undesirable 'conditions'. The report had recommended the establishment of A British Homeland Development Agency 'to prepare for the day when apartheid comes to an end' and to win African goodwill in the interim.

The amounts voted for 1974-75 (as amended in the Supplementary Estimates) were:

	Annual grant R	Additional grant R	Supplementary amount R	Total R
Transkei	16,568,000	44,227,000	3,222,700	64,017,700
Ciskei	6,282,000	12,399,000	2,115,600	20,796,600
Kwa Zulu	19,767,000	36,410,000	3,884,000	60,061,000
BophuthaTswana	7,464,000	18,800,000	2,665,000	28,929,000
Lebowa	7,691,000	14,328,000	1,951,400	23,970,400
Venda	3,198,000	4,847,000	1,024,500	9,069,500
Gazankulu	2,457,000	5,731,000	1,093,000	9,281,000
Basotho Qwaqwa	—	1,815,000	372,100	2,187,100
	63,427,000	138,557,000	16,328,300	218,312,300

COLOURED AFFAIRS

The Government's policy towards the Coloured community was thrown into confusion in 1974; it produced a crisis within the Government (see Politics above) and a direct confrontation between the Government and the Coloured leaders. The Government's own proteges in the Federal Party began to reject the efficacy of the Coloured Representative Council (CRC), set up in 1969 as an advisory 'parliament'.[101] The Federal Party's Transvaal congress in April 1974 recommended abolition of the CRC. The Federal Party (a number of its representatives are

Government nominees) thus moved towards Coloured Labour Party's long-held view that there should be nothing less than total and direct representation of Coloured people in the white Parliament.

The Labour leader, Sonny Leon, introduced a motion in the CRC in July 1974 declaring that it had no confidence in Separate Development and that there should be direct representation in the white Parliament 'as a prelude to the enfranchisement of all South Africans'. The motion was carried by 29 votes to 25. Some Federal Party members supported it, and others abstained. This vote produced a period of confusion while the now dominant Labour Party insisted that the CRC should be immediately abolished. On 29 July the Federal Party leader, Tom Swartz, led a walk-out of his members and said they would return only to listen to a statement from the Minister for Coloured Relations proroguing the CRC. The Prime Minister called in Leon and Swartz and, according to Leon,[102] offered him the chairmanship of the CRC executive 'should Mr Swartz resign'. Leon replied that he would not 'sell' his principles or his people.

Determined to show its unwavering resolve, the Government issued a succession of statements affirming that while the National Party was in power the Coloured people would never be represented in Parliament, directly or indirectly. The Minister of Interior told a SWA National Party congress[103] that the policy for Coloureds was 'parallel development' as distinct from Separate Development, and that parallel lines could never meet. On 19 August, after a four-hour meeting between the Prime Minister, the Minister for Coloured Relations, the secretary of the CRC and six members of the Labour Party, the Prime Minister said[104] he was not prepared to accept the CRC motion calling for its own abolition and for Coloured representation in Parliament. He believed the future of the Coloured people lay in the use and development of the CRC with extended powers. He believed that two Parliaments could exist in one land and he foresaw a 'statutory body' consisting of white and Coloured parliamentary members. Leon replied[105] that the Labour Party would continue to press for full parliamentary representation and the rejection of Separate Development and the CRC. However, he mollified his position somewhat by saying that since nothing but 'parallel development' could be expected from the present Government his party's immediate programme would be to press for socio-economic parity, especially in housing, education and employment. In the long term, however, he added, the Government and the Coloured people were 'on a collision course'. Another meeting between the Prime Minister and a Coloured delegation (from both CRC parties) took place in early September. Afterwards the PM indicated: '(a) that there were specific areas in which the interests of the Coloureds were dominant, and should accordingly be managed entirely by the CRC; (b) that there were similarly specific areas in which the interests of the whites were dominant and had to be handled exclusively by Parliament; (c) that there were areas affecting the mutual interests of both white and brown in which the Coloureds should also have a say on matters affecting Coloured interests.' He suggested alternative joint bodies for this purpose. After this meeting Swartz recommended continuing contact and dialogue and welcomed the right of Coloureds to be involved in statutory bodies; but Leon said the discussions amounted to complete rejection of the Coloured people, adding: 'I am not interested in further window-dressing talks with the Prime Minister . . . We now have no alternative but to go to those people whose arms are open to us—the black people of SA.'

At the commencement of the second session of the CRC on 11 November, Tom Swartz became seriously ill and had to retire. The Labour Party meanwhile pressed for rejection of the Prime Minister's proposals.

The Budget allocation from the Department of Coloured Relations and Rehoboth

Affairs for year ending 31 March 1975 was: provisions for CRC R 132,993,000; salaries of 1,292 educational personnel seconded to the CRC R 6,475,000.

The Theron Commission appointed in 1973 to inquire into the efforts of the Coloured Community[106] was expected to complete its report some time in 1975.

INDIAN AFFAIRS

The life of the first SA Indian Council, which has only limited advisory powers, expired in August 1974. The reconstituted Council consists of 30 members, half Government-nominated and half elected by members of Indian local authorities and consultative and management committees. Elections took place in November. Powers delegated to the new Council cover education and community welfare. The Council's former chairman, H. E. Joosub, said that Indians would not be satisfied with such limited powers and were unhappy with the system of voting. The Indian Management Committee of Lenasia (Johannesburg) boycotted the elections and declared that the election method was 'an affront to the dignity and the citizenship rights of the Indian people'.

At the first meeting of the new Indian Council on 29 November the Prime Minister bluntly warned them that confrontation with the Government would get them nowhere; the Government was determined on multi-nationalism. While aware of the dissatisfaction with the present set-up of the Council it should be considered as only a phase in the development towards the Indians getting the same status as the Coloureds. Eventually there would be a Cabinet Council to liaise with the CRC and the advanced Indian Council, with representation by the two communities on statutory boards. But the chairman of the Indian Council, A. M. Moola, asked what had happened to Dr Verwoerd's promise of 12 years before that the Indians would be accepted as belonging to the white part of SA where they would be given their rights.

STUDENT AND UNIVERSITY AFFAIRS

The Afrikaanse Studentebond (ASB) remained aloof from all other student organizations. Its leaders said they saw little prospect of meaningful contact with the National Union of SA Students (Nusas) or the SA Student Organization (Saso) because of fundamental differences of approach: for Afrikaans students there could be no departure from the framework of Separate Development.

Nusas continued its fight to maintain its identity under persistent Government action against it.[107] The affected Organizations Bill was introduced in Parliament in February 1974 following the Schlebusch Commission's interim reports of 1973. Nusas was referred to, along with the SA Institute of Race Relations and the Christian Institute, as 'active in the extra-parliamentary political field, in co-operation with foreign organizations and people that were trying to achieve their own political ends'. The Schlebusch Commission's final report on Nusas,[108] ran to 641 pages and referred to the student body as an effective power base for a small 'leader clique and their fellow-travellers'. A leadership training programme had aimed at producing 'student radicals imbued with left-wing views'. This small group of radicals undertook 'political indoctrination of young people in their formative years', propagated anti-SA views and promoted anti-SA action. Nusas leaders were also accused of promoting Black Consciousness and favouring a policy based on polarity of black and white in SA, leading to confrontation. The general body of students were stated to have had very little knowledge, or only a superficial knowledge, of the activities of the 'leadership clique'. The Commission recommended that measures be taken 'to prevent political activities in SA from being supported and influenced by financial help from abroad', and 'to combat subversion of the State' by people encouraging arms boycotts against SA as part of an attempt to bring about radical change in the existing political order. The Commission particularly urged that Nusas should be prevented from having a system of centre affiliations. Of the Commission's ten members there was dissent by the three members of the UP who recommended explicit detail in Parliament for any preventive legal action contemplated by the Government and also dissociated themselves from the Government's banning orders served on Nusas leaders in 1973.

The Government declared Nusas an 'Affected Organization' on 13 September. It also declared three subsidiary bodies—Nused, Nuswel and Aquarius—as being 'affected'. They were thus cut off from any sources of foreign aid.

The Nusas president-elect, Karel Tip, disclosed[109] that c. 70% of Nusas' budget (c. R100,000 in 1973) had been obtained from overseas. Nusas described the Government action as part of a concerted drive to eliminate opposition to policies of discrimination and domination. 'What is being attacked is the right of students, of young people, to determine what is wrong with their society and to embark on creative programmes to counter its ills and to open the possibility for a positive future. These programmes, like literacy training, prison education, and community development, are conceived by students. The funds which are now being denied us have always been raised and spent on our terms.' Nusas decided to intensify efforts to raise money from local sources for its continuing programmes.

In April Nusas recorded its 'grave reservations' about the electoral and parliamentary process in SA, noting that less than one-quarter of the population was entitled to cast a vote and that no white political party had committed itself to an egalitarian society. It branded all the parliamentary parties as 'white supremacist', but nevertheless recommended eligible students to vote in the elections with the aim of 'replacing as many backward-looking members with as many forward-looking members as possible'.

Nusas launched a campaign for the release of political prisoners and of those who were banned and detained 'for active opposition to apartheid and white domination'. When students at Witswatersrand University were refused permission to stage a march through Johannesburg, they held a demonstration at the edge of the campus which resulted in a clash with police.

Nusas' 51st annual congress in July decided on a change of strategy. As its public protests appeared to have accomplished little it would concentrate on practical activities, including prison education, wage investigations and literacy projects. It thus abolished its educational branch (Nused) and welfare department (Nuswel) leaving students on individual campuses to carry on these activities. The Nusas publication *Dissent* (March/April 1974) published an article on 'Black Consciousness' which concentrated on the necessity of whites to liberate themselves from racism, a process described as 'long and difficult . . . It requires firstly an awareness of precisely how deeply racism has permeated our concepts of reality and our identity. Emotionally and intellectually one has to go through a long period of critical self-examination to understand the forces that have shaped us—this process of desocialization and de-colonization is a total process as it involves re-discovering the history of our country and culture of its peoples. The difficulty here lies in developing a balanced response to these "discoveries" as it is all too easy to develop exaggerated feelings of collective guilt.' The November issue of *Dissent* prominently featured events in Mozambique, publishing extracts from Samora Machel's speech on the investiture of the Mozambique Provisional Government and reporting on new contacts between Nusas and the Mozambique students' body AAM.

The founder of Nusas in 1924, and its honorary president, Leo Marquard, died at the end of March. In September, Nusas' banned former president, Neville Curtis, applied for political asylum in Australia having left SA secretly.

A Government commission which was set up to report on apartheid in SA's Universities posed a further threat to the English-language Universities' 'cosmopolitan' character. The commission proposed increased governmental control of finances and overall supervision. The commission rejected the belief, put forward by the English-language Universities, that they should be free to make academic appointments from the best qualified people without regard to race, colour or creed. In a minority report Prof. G. R. Bozzoli, Principal of Witwatersrand University, said that certain chapters of the report were 'an attack on the English-language universities', and amounted to a 'proposal to bring all the universities into conformity with Government policy as interpreted by the Government presently in power'. Nusas leaders attacked the Commission's recommendations.

Despite continued arrests and banning of its leaders, the Black Students' Organization (Saso) remained in existence. At its sixth General Council in July it condemned the 'growing false feeling of relevance of Homeland leaders, the Coloured Representative Council and SA Indian Council in black politics'. (Also see sections on Black Politics and Detentions and Bannings.)

DEFENCE AND SECURITY

SA's defence expenditure showed another substantial increase in 1974, to over R700 m—almost 40% more than in 1973. Justifying the rise,[110] the Minister of Defence, P. W. Botha, said that it had been decided to complete the Defence Force's ten-year budget plan in five years. Costs of armaments had 'sky-rocketed'. SA had become self-sufficient in many spheres of armanents' manufacture, 'but we are still compelled by the time factor to buy items direct from producers where this is economical'. Provision for the purchase of arms rose by R134 m to R312 m, and expenditure for 'landward defence' almost doubled from R161 m to c. R293 m. Expenditure on air defence rose from R44 m to R62 m. Maritime defence went up from R28 m to c. R56 m.

A significant break with tradition came in 1974 when the first Africans were recruited for the Defence Force. According to military spokesmen,[111] recruits would be trained in drill, military law, handling weapons, first aid and hygiene. They would subsequently be employed mainly on guard duties but also as drivers, clerks, storemen and dog handlers. Defence Force spokenmen said[112] that discussions had taken place between the Government and some Homeland leaders on the setting up of defence forces for the Homelands. These forces would be lined up with SA forces should border warfare ever reach the intensity of Portuguese-Frelimo clashes in Mozambique. Authorities were quoted as saying that if black SA soldiers were to be 'properly motivated for anti-terrorist operations' efforts would have to be made to eliminate the political and economic disabilities imposed on them under present Government policies. The acting head of the army, Maj-Gen. J. R. Dutton, said[113] that black soldiers would be 'integrated' into the defence force in terms of government policy. A black driver would be allowed to drive a truck filled with white soldiers. There were no plans to create a black officer corps 'but this is possible with time'. At present blacks could advance to the rank of Sgt-Maj. Class 1. This would take 'a good soldier' about nine years. By the end of 1974 48 blacks were being trained. They were reviewed on 4 December by Chief Matanzima who said that never before had danger from outside approached so closely to the borders of SA: 'All of us must be prepared to defend ourselves; we must stand together, all groups, all races, and all Homelands.' Increased 'border defence' was foreseen by the Minister of Police in October who announced details of a volunteer police corps to take over all police duties on the borders. He also announced additional allowances and bonuses for SA police in Rhodeşia. He described these steps as essential because 'combating terrorism in Rhodesia necessitated the use of weapons of war and was to an increasing extent becoming a sort of conventional warfare'.

According to the Director-General of Strategic Studies for the SA Defence Force[114] Maj-Gen. J. H. Robbertze, the 'terrorist threat' remained real as long as there were bases and sanctuaries in neighbouring countries. In an obvious reference to Mozambique, he said the 'terrorist threat' could not be pinned down to merely an abhorrent action of a common criminal—the problem was 'not so simple'. Many Governments of independent States today had been 'representative of terrorists yesterday'. He added: 'They are recognized and accepted by world society. They sit in the highest international gatherings on the basis of one-man, one-vote.' On the same occasion the Director of Army Operations, Brig. C. L. Viljoen, said the consolidation of the Homelands was beneficial to the defence of SA. Fragmentation of the Homelands was unacceptable from a military point of view. The retiring head of the air force, Lt. Gen. J. P. Verster, said[115] that the SA air force was one of the most formidable on the African continent. It had the most modern armaments available in the 'free world'; the hundreds of millions of rands taxpayers had contributed to date had been 'invested effectively' for the protection of SA. However, the Director General of the SAAF Supporting Services, Maj-Gen. Tom Cockbain, said there were a number of deadly weapons available to black Africa which were 'very worrying'. The deadliest was the Russian SAM 7, which the Portuguese had encountered. Another was the Russian anti-aircraft gun. Also the Russian SAM 2, 3 and 6 missiles were 'very nasty and widely deployed' in Africa. These weapons 'could lose us a lot of aircraft'. One of the problems in a possible conflict between SA and Black Africa was that 'there are not an awful lot of really rewarding targets for our aircraft'; in contrast, SA had more rewarding targets for Black African aircraft. He said the air defence situation had 'deteriorated' over the past ten years, during which time Black Africa had acquired Mirages and MiGs.

The Minister of Defence announced in July that Salisbury Island, Durban, would be re-established as a fully operational naval base and would also be the headquarters for an Indian Service Battalion, for which recruiting would start shortly. It was also announced that Simonstown naval base would be extensively expanded for the first time since it was built in the early years of the century. The Defence Minister hinted that licences had been obtained abroad to build certain classes of naval vessels locally.[116] He was probably referring to the long-deferred construction of six naval corvettes of Portuguese design, reports of which had been circulating for some years.

After Britain's decision to abrogate the Simonstown Agreement[117] the SA Government stressed that Simonstown and all other military facilities in SA were still available to Britain and other friendly countries in the West. NATO Defence Ministers were also quoted as saying privately[118] that the defence of the Cape sea route was 'well-covered' in a contingency plan and that SA would receive naval assistance if the oil route were threatened.

A Defence Bill imposing compulsory compliance with military service and massive fines or 10 years' imprisonment on anyone who encourages anyone else not to perform military service passed its second reading in Parliament at the end of August. The SA Council of Churches and the Roman Catholic bishops had earlier said that it was not automatically the duty of Christians to engage in violence and war or to prepare to do so whenever the State demanded. They now warned that the Bill could create a new generation of Christian martyrs (see Religion below). The UP unanimously supported the Bill since the party was 'at one with the Government on the defence of the sovereignty of the State'; but the Progressives said that the Government had over-reacted to the SACC's resolution. Chief Lucas Mangope of

BophuthaTswana commented[119] that if the proposed clause outlawing conscientious objection became law it would be very difficult for Homeland leaders to put their case to their people that the volunteering for military service should be conditional on being given a real stake in SA. He went on: 'We are prepared to lay down our lives in defence of our country, but life is sacred . . . We do not want anybody to get the impression that we are to defend the country for the privileged position of others and the disabilities and inequalities that we are subjected to.' Similar views were expressed by Chief Buthelezi, Sonny Leon and Cedric Phatudi. During the third reading debate the Minister accepted a UP amendment to reduce the maximum penalties for inciting a person not to serve in the Defence Force. He said that genuine conscientious objectors could serve in non-combatant positions without weapons even if they did not belong to recognized pacifist churches. He added that he was willing to meet Church leaders to discuss the measure.

Total armed forces: 15,700 regular, 31,750 conscripts. Defence expenditure: 1974-75: 500 million rand ($750 million).

The Army of 7,000 regular, 27,500 conscripts (some SA troops are operating in the Caprivi Strip) comprises 3 infantry brigades, each of 1 tank, 1 infantry and 1 artillery battalion, 100 Centurion Mark 5, 20 Comet medium tanks; 1,000 AML-60 and AML-90 and 50 M-3 armed cars; 50 Ferret scout cars; 250 Saracen, about 100 V-150 Commando APC; 25 powder gun/howitzers, 155 mm howitzers; 35 mm L-70/40 and 3.7 inch AA guns. 3 batteries of 18 Cactus (Crotale) SAM.

The reserves comprise 60,000 Citizen Force, in 9 territorial commands. Reservists serve 9 days a year for 9 years.

The navy consists of 3,200 regular, 1,250 conscripts and has 3 submarines, 2 destroyers with Wasp ASW helicopters, 6 ASW frigates (3 with Wasp ASW helicopters), 1 escort minesweeper (training ship), 10 coastal minesweepers, 5 seaward defence boats, 1 fleet replenishment tanker, 7 Wasp helicopters (10 more on order).

Reserves: 9,000 trained reserves in Citizen Force (with 2 frigates and 7 minesweepers).

The air force of 5,500 regular and 3,000 conscripts has about 100 combat aircraft, 1 bomber squadron with 6 Canberra B(I) Mk 12, 3 T Mk 4, 1 light bomber squadron with 10 Buccaneer S Mk 50, 2 fighter squadrons with 32 Mirage IIIEZ and 8 IIIDZ, 1 fighter/recce squadron with 16 Mirage IIICZ, 4 IIIBZ and 4 IIIRZ, 2 MR squadrons with 7 Shackleton MR3, 9 Piaggio P-166S Albatross)11 more P-166S on order) 4 transport squadrons with 7 C-130B, 9 Transall C-190Z, 23 C-47, 5 C-54, 1 Viscount 781 and 4 HS-125 Mercurius, 4 helicopter squadrons: two with 20 Alouette III each; one with 20 SA-330 Puma; one with 15 SA-32L Super Frelon (one flight of 7 Wasp naval-assigned), (1 army-assigned light aircraft squadron with Cessna 185A/D and A185E to be replaced by AM-3C.), Trainers including Harvard; 160 MB-326M Impala (some armed in a COIN role); Vampire FB Mk 6, Mk 9, T Mk 55; TF-86; C-47 and Alouette II/III, (15 MB-326K on order.)

Reserves: 3,000 Active Citizen Force. 8 squadrons with 20 Impala; 100 Harvard IIA, III, T-6G (Texan); 20 Cessna 185A/D, A185E. 12 Air Commando squadrons (private aircraft).

Para-Military Forces: 75,000 Commandoes organized and trained as a Home-Guard.

INDUSTRIAL AFFAIRS
TROUBLE IN THE MINES

SA's most serious new industrial threat surfaced on the gold and coal mines in 1974 when for the first time in a century the mining companies had to face the prospect of not being able to recruit sufficient labour. Harry Oppenheimer and other mining leaders repeatedly warned of the seriousness of this development (see the Republic's Future above). The mines absorb 300,000 workers—all migrants on 18 months' contracts. Although gold mining is SA's most profitable industry it was, until 1974, its lowest paying. In real terms, wages actually went down between 1911 and 1973.[120] Starting with the Carletonville shootings in September 1973[121] a wave of protest and violence swept through the gold mines causing 58 deaths and hundreds of injuries by the end of 1974. One serious repercussion of this conflict was the departure of tens of thousands of alien black workers. The Chamber of Mines and its principal members were compelled to propose a number of new measures to prevent the industry being totally disrupted. These included higher wages, recruitment of urban and rural workers from 'white' SA; some mining leaders even wanted to recognize black trade unions, to which the Chamber of Mines had been resolutely opposed throughout its history.

Malawi, a major source of mine labour, banned recruitment of its workers in 1974; while workers from Lesotho and Mozambique began to withdraw voluntarily. In their place the SA authorities had to look seriously at the home labour market for the first time. *Radio Bantu* began broadcasting advertisements that went: 'Let's go to the mines, Joe, there's no money here.' 'No man, four years ago I was a miner. The work was hard.' 'But it's a man's work. Today miners get double the pay and a clever man can save R500 a year.' Recruitment in Rhodesia was also allowed for the first time. The changing situation is illustrated by the following chart indicating the sources of black miners:

	Oct. 1973	%	Oct. 1974	%
SA	79,120	21	78,024	24
Lesotho	74,766	20	69,014	21
Botswana	17,614	5	13,616	4
Swaziland	4,139	1	4,755	2
Malawi (and tropical countries)	109,789	30	79,745	24
Mozambique	86,171	23	82,509	25
Total	371,599	100	327,663	100

Source: SA Chamber of Mines

The drop in labour meant that the mines were operating with only 78% of their requirements of black underground workers and the position was expected to get worse. The main loss was from Malawi. In April 1974, President Banda suspended all recruiting after 77 Malawians were killed in an air crash in a recruiting company's plane. By December over 1,600 black miners were returning to Malawi each week without being replaced. 45,000 had returned since April.

Violence in the mines was generally directed against the management but also assumed inter-tribal dimensions caused by the frustrations of men living bachelor lives in close quarters. In February 1974, 23 men were killed and 106 injured in fighting between Basotho and Xhosas at three Anglo-American mines. It led to the departure of 60% of the employees at the Free State Geduld mine, 47% at Welkom and 34% at Western Holdings. A total of 15,000 workers went home to Lesotho. Further fighting broke out at Western Deep Levels in April leaving 10 dead and 30 wounded. More Basotho returned home. By this time Anglo-American was already talking about a 'serious loss of production' following the disturbances. The 'Harmony' gold mine in the Orange Free State was the scene of a major riot over wage claims on 9 June. Four miners were killed in a clash with police. In October c. 1,400 Malawians at the Western Deep Levels refused to go underground and demanded to be repatriated after one of their countrymen was stabbed to death, while at the ERPM mine at Germiston c. 1,000 Mozambicans went on strike for higher wages after security forces' attempts to break up their protests. A wage claim disturbance at the Hartebeestfontein mine at Stilfontein led to the deaths of two miners. After four days of strikes at the mine, involving c. 11,000 miners, there was a reluctant return to work there.

In January 1975 there was renewed turmoil, chiefly involving Basotho workers protesting against their own Government's new regulations deferring their pay. Eight men were killed, 33 injured and at one stage 12,000 were on strike. Thousands asked for repatriation. On 15 January, Anglo-American summarily dismissed 2,400 for striking and attempting to incite other workers to join their action. Their dismissal was in line with a directive from the Chamber of Mines that 'trouble-makers' would automatically be sent home. The January 1975 disturbances appeared to be more immediately related to Lesotho politics than to conditions in the mines; but the fact that so many preferred repatriation in their poverty-stricken Homeland to working in the mines showed a complete disenchantment with the industry. The Chamber of Mines' first proposal to deal with the new situation was a crash programme of research and development, with emphasis on mechanization.[122] The Chamber's president, A. W. S. Schumann, said the recent pay increases offered to African workers had meant their labour was becoming 'uneconomic'. He continued to defend migrant labour, although Anglo-American (the largest employer in the mining industry) was in favour of stabilizing its work force.

The Chamber announced two pay increases for black miners during 1974. From 1 December the minimum starting pay for novice underground workers in gold and coal mines rose from R1.20 to R1.60 a shift, while the starting rate for surface workers rose from R1.00 to R1.20 a shift. The rate for underground novices had thus more than trebled in 18 months. Anglo-American and the 'more progressive' mining houses had pressed for even more, but a compromise was reached between them and the 'conservative' Gold Fields and Anglovaal. Anglo-American also went further than its competitors in announcing its willingness to recognize and negotiate with African trade unions in all its enterprises.[123] Its only proviso was that black unions should be run by 'responsible people' who could show they were fully representative. Its chairman, Harry Oppenheimer, told a conference in Johannesburg at the end of July that strikes by African workers posed an increasing threat to SA industry, and that African workers' consciousness of their potential strength was building up daily. 'Black workers are increasingly aware of the power of the strike weapon, and it is quite certain that if better means of settling disputes cannot be evolved, this weapon will be used more and more.' He called for a multi-racial commission of inquiry to put forward a plan for the effective representation of all workers in trade unions.

The Government, for its part, took steps to ease the mining industry's dependence on foreign African labour. In November 1974 it eased regulations inhibiting the recruitment of urban Africans to work in the mines. Hitherto, Government regulations obliged urban Africans to return to their supposed 'Homeland of origin' on completion of their contracts for the mining companies. It was now agreed that miners could return to the area from which they are recruited. In November, too, the Chamber of Mines, announced a major policy switch. 'From today,' its president said, 'we must cease to think in terms of a black labour force which will continue indefinitely to be migratory and unskilled.'[124] The chairman of the 'Johnnies' Mining group, Sir Albert Robinson, proposed the development of a non-discriminatory, trained and stable labour force open to all races. 'The ultimate goal,' he said, 'is a uniform wage scale for all employees, irrespective of race, based on objective criteria.' By the end of 1974 it seemed that the Government's position had come closer to that of the hard-headed economic realists in SA's business community than it had ever been before.

STRIKES AND TRADE UNIONS

The unrest and violence on the mines was part of a developing pattern of unrest among all African industrial workers, warned the director of the SA Institute of Race Relations, Fred van Wyk, in June 1974.[125] He added that the Government would have to act swiftly to create working and living conditions acceptable to Africans, and to lift them out of the conditions of dire poverty in which most of their families were living. 'We are sitting on a powder keg unless these factors are recognized, and efforts are made to eliminate them,' he added.

Since the strike wave by black workers started in late 1972,[126] there had been well over 300 illegal strikes by black workers by the end of 1974. One experienced observer[127] noted that the new climate of rising expectations was 'constantly being recharged by the spirals of inflation, and the truth is now dawning on white employers that a process has been started that can never be stopped'. He added: 'The industrial unrest in SA will get worse unless black workers are allowed to form trade unions.'

The overall effect of the wave of strikes was to show that the 1973 Bantu Labour Act was unworkable.[128] Arthur Grobbelaar, general-secretary of the Trade Union Council of SA (Tucsa), described the Act and the concept of works committees as 'inadequate', 'ineffective' and 'futile'.[129] The works committees were 'looked upon with distrust and suspicion and cannot adequately convey the aspirations of African workers'. He added that African workers should have bargaining power through recognized worker representation. This, too, was the view of a Homeland representative who had played an active role in settling disputes in Durban during the year. Barney Dladla (former KwaZulu Executive Councillor for Community Affairs) declared:[130] 'The works committees will never work effectively. African workers want a real say in their affairs. If they could have this they would not resort to strikes.' These views were echoed by a significant number of white employers. A movement among employers to recognize and negotiate with black unions, despite Government opposition, was given a boost by a wage agreement between Smith and Nephew (a British subsidiary) and an African textile union—the first such agreement in SA.

The majority of African workers, however, remained without any formal organization at all, whether in works committees or unofficial trade unions. By June 1974 there were only 1,050 liaison committees and 175 works committees in existence, although SA has c. 30,000 factories. Similarly, the lack of official status for black unions meant that in 1974 there were only about a dozen in existence, with a membership of less than 30,000 workers—out of an economically active black population of 5.5 m. Despite pressure from many quarters the Minister of Labour, Marais Viljoen, refused to change his position. On a number of occasions during 1974 he said that works and liaison committees gave African workers 'all the scope they needed at present'. In a major statement[131] he declared: 'The Government does not intend reviewing again the organizing of black workers, and believes that it is in the interests of all concerned to maintain the *status quo*.' He said that if black unions were recognized it would cause an 'uprising' among whites. White trade unions would be swamped by blacks. He added: 'As everybody is aware, trade unions have become a major political force in the world. They are no longer merely wage and service negotiating instruments. In many countries they have assumed the role of Government-makers or breakers.'

Meanwhile Tucsa at its conference in Port Elizabeth in September voted overwhelmingly to re-open its membership to African trade unions. Significantly, this move was not as controversial as it might have been a year earlier, but it was not greeted with particular enthusiasm by African workers' representatives. Those present at the conference declared that membership of Tucsa was 'not the fundamental problem faced by the workers of SA.' More important was the nature of future relationships between registered white unions and black unions. Attempts by whites to assist Africans to form their own unions received a setback when the Government imposed banning orders on four white members of Mrs Harriet Bolton's taskforce organizing African workers. This veteran trade union champion decided to emigrate. By the end of 1974 four organizations were involved in helping workers to organize themselves: the Industrial Aid Society (Johannesburg); the Institute for Industrial Education (Durban); Central Administration Services (Durban); and the Western Province Workers' Advice Bureau (Cape Town). All reported that black trade union activities were being closely scrutinized by police agents.[132] The Institute for Industrial Education received a grant of R18,000 from the British Trades Union Council (TUC) in December. A TUC spokesman said the grant would be followed by more aid to groups promoting trade unionism among black South Africans.

LABOUR POLICY

Job Reservation—whereby certain categories of employment could be reserved exclusively for whites in times of unemployment—continued to be eroded. The Minister of Labour, Marais Viljoen, revealed[133] that the 'shortage of white workers' has been 60,000 in 1973 and would be 82,000 in 1977. This meant, he said, that 5,000 blacks would be taking over 'white jobs' every year. The manufacturing industry alone was creating 57,000 more jobs a year; of these 11,700 would be filled by Coloureds and 37,800 by Africans. In this situation, he added, employers had to bear in mind the necessity of paying 'decent wages', of effective training, and of 'healthy relations' between employers and workers. Figures released by the Department of Statistics[134] showed that two-thirds of the labour force in Government departments, provincial administrations and local authorities were black workers. They also revealed that the numbers of black workers were increasing faster than those of whites—a trend apparent throughout the economy, private as well as public. The figures further showed the continuing gap between black and white earnings in the public sector—260,000 whites earned R300 m while 416,000 blacks earned R 124 m.

SA Railways, a bastion of job reservation, found itself having to give over still more 'white jobs' to blacks during 1974. For the first time blacks were being trained as truck drivers in Port Elizabeth. The shift of blacks from unskilled to semi-skilled jobs was also accelerating in the engineering industry, according to the Steel and Engineering Industries Federation of SA.[135] Their survey showed a substantial movement in the past six years of black employment upward into higher grade work, and also into occupations previously filled by whites. J. P. Coetzee, the general manager of Iscor, the State-owned steel corporation, said[136] that blacks had to be trained in all aspects of the industry, 'otherwise whites would in the future have to train blacks in the industry in their own Homelands.' He admitted that the white labour shortage had reached a critical stage at Iscor: 'If the present tendencies continue the shortage of white labour by 1984 at Iscor will total 7,300. Already many men are working seven-day weeks as well as 12-hour shifts.'

Despite such pessimistic statements the Government was still unwilling to ease job reservation in some areas. One engineering firm—headed by a National Party MP—was ordered to stop employing Africans as welders as this contravened Government regulations.

One of the Government's more positive moves in 1974 was the repeal of the anachronistic Masters and Servants Act of 1856 which governed employment conditions of farm labourers and domestic workers throughout the country. The Act had made it an imprisonable offence for a servant to leave his master's service without permission. In 1973 there had been more than 17,000 prosecutions under the Act. This decision was taken after American labour unions protesting against coal imports from SA had cited the 'slave labour' nature of the Masters and Servants Act in a petition to the US Courts.

The Government also repealed Section 15 of the Bantu Labour Act, making it a criminal offence for a black contract miner to break his conditions of employments. This section had been proved to be unworkable by events on the mines in 1974.

EMPLOYMENT

A speech by Senator Owen Horwood, Minister of Economic Affairs, in August to the effect that SA had no unemployment problem, only a problem of under-employment, produced a number of reactions in the form of estimates of the present situation. Only unemployed whites, Coloureds and Asians are registered; in 1974 registered unemployment in these groups was very low, rising slightly towards the end of the year. But the African unemployed are not registered. The 1970 census gave a figure of 283,000 for Africans unemployed. However, it also said that 3.67 m African men and 5.76 m African women were 'not economically active'. If the number of people below 15 and over 64 are subtracted from these totals, there were 253,000 men and 2.22 m women classed as 'not economically active'—in addition to the 'unemployed'. Professor J. L. Sadie of Stellenbosch pointed out (*Financial Mail*, 30 August, 1974) that with African incomes as low as they are, it is realistic to assume that most of the 'not economically active' of both sexes are in fact involuntarily unemployed. He also showed that many of the Africans classified in the census as economically active are in fact only seasonally active; and many more who are simply eking out a living on an inadequate plot in a Homeland are described as 'employed in the agricultural sector'.

The Economics Departments of three Afrikaans Universities—the Orange Free State, Stellenbosch and Pretoria—all of which produced separate results of research into African employment in 1974 came to roughly the same conclusion: that African unemployment is rising by c. 100,000 every year, even when there is virtually no unemployment in the other racial groups. The calculation is based on the fact that c. 105,000 Africans come onto the labour market from the 'Homelands' every year, and c. 98,000 from the 'white' urban areas. About 100,000 are absorbed into jobs every year. Only about a sixth of Homeland recruits to the labour market can be employed in a Homeland or a 'border area'.

The Chief Minister of the Ciskei Homeland, commenting on Senator Horwood's remark, said that 'more than half' the Africans in the Ciskei are unemployed: 'Senator Horwood speaks from ignorance: if he came to the Ciskei he would see his ignorance,' he said. Arthur Grobbelaar, Tucsa's general secretary, said he could only think the Minister had access to secret information. 'Otherwise he is talking through his hat . . . '

The Christian Institute, in a new publication *White Immigration to South Africa* estimates that at current rates of growth there will be 728,000 unemployed by 1975, virtually all of them black. The Institute calls for an end to white immigration designed to fill jobs with foreign whites. It points out, for example, that Africans are excluded from skilled jobs in most of the building industry, while white foreigners are recruited to meet the shortage of building artisans. A Johannesburg municipality proposal to employ Coloured bus drivers was turned down by the Government, which then tried to recruit bus drivers in Britain.

The Steel and Engineering Industries Federation of SA announced a pilot immigration scheme in October under which it hopes to recruit 1,000 white artisans from abroad. The scheme has the co-operation of the Department of Immigration, which finances assistance to the families of recruited workers.

In January 1975 the first of several training centres for black industrial workers in the 'white' urban areas opened its doors. The centres represent a concession by the Government to critics of the policy of cheap, low-productivity labour, and to the rising demand for a stable, trained labour force. Tax concessions were made to private industry to encourage it to make its contribution to training black workers: for every R1,000 spent by a private firm on training, R2,000 is deductable from taxable income, and R2,250 if the training project is in a 'development area'.

EMPLOYMENT IN SELECTED SECTORS, DECEMBER 1973

	Africans	Whites	Coloureds	Asians
Mining and Quarrying	596,374	61,371	6,749	518
Manufacturing	696,700	279,400	213,400	78,700
Electricity	17,400	10,400	600	—
Construction	278,200	59,700	48,000	54,000
Railways and Harbours	102,822	106,829	16,474	1,311
Post Office	16,145	40,311	5,052	678
Provincial Administrators	81,640	100,705	16,299	2,516
Local Authorities	22,190	54,457	6,541	1,207

Source: SA Bulletin of Statistics, June 1974.

WAGES

Despite wage gains by Africans there was no evidence in 1974 of any serious closing of the discriminatory gap in earnings between the races. According to surveys by the University of SA's Bureau of Market Research[137] the incomes of urban Africans were increasing at a slower rate than those of Coloureds and Indians, and much slower than those of whites.

The Johannesburg *Financial Mail*[138] alleged Government secretiveness over public sector pay increases because the evidence did not bear out its claim to be narrowing the racial pay gap. SA Railways, for example, had maintained that white pay increases were in line with the current rate of inflation while non-white increases were 'greater than the rate of inflation, resulting automatically in a higher purchasing power for non-whites and therefore a relative narrowing in the wage gap'. But the *Financial Mail* pointed out that an African earning R100 a month who gets a 15% increase is no nearer closing the gap even when his white counterpart on R400 a month gets an increase of only 10%. The black ends up with R115 and the white with $440. The gap is thus *increased* from R300 to R325.

Meanwhile, academics were still looking at ways of defining Poverty Datum Lines (PDL), Minimum Effective Levels (MEL) and Minimum Living Levels (MLL) without reaching agreement. The Government was in no apparent hurry to establish a national minimum wage. Researchers at the University of Port Elizabeth did however record disturbing findings about the rate of inflation and its effect on minimum income requirements.[139] Between October 1973 and October 1974 there were sharp increases of between 18% and 25%.

In Britain, a House of Commons committee in March published its report on wages and conditions of Africans employed by British companies in SA after a nine-month investigation.[140] The report suggested that those British companies which could not afford to pay wages above the PDL should pull out of SA. It proposed a 'code of conduct'. The Labour Government accepted the report and promised amplified guidance to British firms that minimum wages be 50% above the PDL.

The Secretary for Trade, Peter Shore, wrote to the chairmen of 565 British companies with subsidiaries or associates in SA drawing attention to the guidelines and urging them to follow 'enlightened policies' for the welfare of their African workers. A special consul was appointed to the British Embassy in Johannesburg to monitor the degree of observance of the guidelines. A British White Paper said that companies with subsidiaries in SA would be invited to give public evidence that they were treating their African employees properly, and promised 'further action' to encourage British companies to improve wages and conditions.[141]

SOCIAL AFFAIRS
BLACK URBAN CONDITIONS
The social and economic conditions of the black population of Soweto (Johannesburg's black dormitory town) were reflected in the unchecked crime rate. By the end of 1974, c. 1,000 people had been murdered in Soweto.[142] According to its Divisional Police Commissioner, Brig. Jan Visser, 'the Bantu is his own enemy . . . I do not know why people should behave like this'. Black leaders placed the blame on the Government. Lennox Mlonzi, an Urban Bantu Councillor and leader of the Soweto Progressive Party pointed out:[143] 'If the hooligans of Soweto were terrorists, the Government would have wiped them out overnight. As long as the killings in Soweto do not affect the white population of this country, the Government will be the last to make a noise about such happenings.' Others blamed the social conditions—poverty, inadequate housing, lack of recreation facilities and inadequate education. One newspaper showed how Soweto's conditions bred crime and hooligans.[144] With its hostels, in which hundreds of men and women are accommodated separately, and its massed 'mini' houses. 'Soweto emerges as little more than a gigantic dormitory for workers'. The two facts most deeply resented were that property and homes cannot be owned or bought, and that when the male breadwinner dies the whole family is evicted from the home. Many blacks referred to Soweto as a 'ghetto' or a 'concentration camp'. The survey revealed that the average house has three or four rooms and is inhabited by six or seven people, often spanning three generations. Only 14% of homes have electricity, 70% have a shower or bath and 3% have running hot water. The biggest problems of Soweto's people were: 'Poverty, the struggle to provide for themselves and their families and, for many of them, the struggle to stay above the breadline; political apartheid in its many facets—pass laws, police raids, influx control and racial discrimination.' Yet 75% of those interviewed felt that Soweto was their home, despite their official designation as 'temporary urban sojourners'. Two-thirds flatly refused to regard the Homelands as their home. One comment was: 'I grew up in Soweto. I cannot imagine any other place as a home . . . I can't imagine going to these sinister areas, places of doom called Bantustans.' Others said: 'Homelands are a deathbed of Africans created by whites. They are barren. If they were fertile they would not be allotted to the Africans.' 'In the Homelands I visualize starvation, disease, unemployment, drought and all that.'

In an interview published in *Deurbraak*, the Progressive Party's Afrikaans magazine,[145] the mayor of Soweto, Peter Lengene, said that dissatisfaction among urban blacks had reached such a pitch that it 'can no longer be controlled'; it was difficult any longer to find 'a so-called moderate black man'. He identified the following major grievances of urban Africans: lack of representation in Parliament, Provincial Councils or Bantu Administration boards; lack of free education and inferior instruction; poor transport and residential facilities; wages not keeping pace with cost of living; disruption of family life.

POPULATION REMOVALS[146]

A study entitled *Uprooting a Nation*[147] estimated that 3 m people had been, or were currently, affected by mass removals under the Government's Separate Development plan. More conservative estimates, based on the Government's own figures, maintained that 1.5 m had been moved and that, by 1980, more than 2 m would have been relocated. Justifying the Government's action, the Deputy Minister of Bantu Administration, Punt Janson, said in July[148] that removal of 'black spots' was in the best long-term interests of SA and that the subject should be taken out of the political arena. He wanted blacks particularly to know that the removals were in the 'ultimate interests of all' and that, as far as possible, they were carried out 'with the greatest consideration for their feelings'. In another statement[149] the Minister suggested that the removal of people was at times 'more unpleasant for the person responsible for the removal' than for the people being moved. He added that his conscience was 'quite clear' that he was doing it 'for a better organized society in which poeple will live happily side by side in their own nations where they can belong, and be more resistant to subversion.'

The most contentious removal in 1974 was that of c. 16,000 'Lebowa citizens' from a farm area near Middelburg. The plan to move them into part of the Lebowa Homeland produced widespread protests (including the Lebowa territorial authority which had not been consulted), as well as from local white farmers (who had depended on the people for their labour). But despite defiance of the police by the victims, all 16,000 were forcibly moved to poorly serviced 'resettlement areas'. The Lebowa Commissioner-General (the SA Government's representative) revealed in July that the Government had plans to move another 130,000 'Lebowa citizens'. Chief G. Ramokgoba, a member of the Lebowa Legislative Assembly, said[150] that his people at Sekgosese had already been moved twice and were now being told to move again. Each move had involved the destruction of his people's homes and 'the theft by the authorities' of donkeys and other animals. Pleas for compensation had been ignored.

Among other mass removals during 1974 were those of 2,000 families from Thaba-Nchu in BophuthaTswana to Tseki in Basotho Qwaqwa (see Homelands above). Press reports showed[151] that several months after the move the 'resettlement area' still had no medical, sanitary or water services. In the Western Cape in February 1,000 villagers were moved to a 'resettlement area' 800 miles to the north in Namibia. In May 150 families of the Banogeng tribe were transported from their ancestral land near Rietfontein in the Western Transvaal to a farm inside BophuthaTswana. Between June and August, 800 Tswana families were moved to BophuthaTswana from trust land at Ventersdorp. It was announced that a new town to replace the Fingo village in Grahamstown was to be built 45 km out of the city; it would accommodate 110,000 people.

The slums of Alexandra township on the northern outskirts of Johannesburg were still being torn down in 1974 to make way for huge single-sex hostels. Although the rebuilding would improve health conditions, it began a new process of family disruption. Husbands were told they could no longer live with their wives and children; in some cases mothers were separated from their children. The Black Sash sent a memorandum to the Minister of Bantu Administration in October, detailing more than 40 cases of families being broken up by the demolition of their houses. Black Sash stressed that the cases they had investigated were only the tip of the iceberg.[152] Rigorous qualifications for family accommodation precluded all widows, divorcees, unmarried mothers, foreigners and those either not born in Alexandra or who had not worked continuously for one employer for 10 years. Black Sash asked for the immediate cessation of demolition of Alexandra as an alternative to the 'unjust, immoral and unchristian' breaking up of families.[153]

EDUCATION

The number of African children at school was expected to exceed 5m by 1980. Between 1972 and 1973 their total number had increased from 3.1m to 3.3m. The Government claimed progress for its programme of providing free books to African school children and increasing the number of teachers. However, an Opposition spokesman in Parliament claimed that African schools were in a 'state of crisis' because of a shortage of teachers and the ban on white teachers in black schools. The discriminatory nature of educational facilities was revealed by the statistics of enrolments at black and white schools and universities respectively. Africans' progress up the educational ladder is severely restricted from primary school onwards to the point that at University level they are outnumbered 28:1 by whites although the black-white population ratio is c. 5:1.

AFRICAN EDUCATION TOTALS, 1972

Area	Schools	Pupils	Teachers	Teacher/pupil ratio
BophuthaTswana	709	292,766	5,006	1.58
Lebowa	822	317,144	5,327	1.59
Basotho Qwaqwa	29	16,575	282	1.58
Ciskei	569	180,157	3,189	1.56
KwaZulu	1,441	472,362	7,856	1.60
Gazankulu	232	84,087	1,268	1.66
Venda	284	81,574	1,381	1.59
Transkei	1,769	456,156	8,091	1.56
Homelands total	5,855	1,900,761	32,400	1.58
White areas	5,093	1,201,060	21,697	1.55
Total SA	10,948	3,101,821	54,097	1.57

Source: Bantu, January 1974.

COMPARATIVE EDUCATION EXPENDITURE 1973-74 (million Rand)

	Revenue account	Loan account
The Provinces (white Education)	371.2	56.7
Department of National Education (mainly white)	123.1	4.4
Department of Coloured Relations	73.4	—
Department of Indian Affairs	32.5	—
Department of Bantu Education	42.2	—
Bantu Homeland Governments	53.8	—
Other State Departments	15.8	16.0
Total	711.9	77.1

Source: Ministry of Statistics.

UNIVERSITY ENROLMENT 1974

University	White	Coloured	Asian	African	Total
Cape Town	8,449	404	113	6	8,972
Durban-Westville	—	—	2,342	—	2,342
Fort Hare	—	—	—	1,029	1,029
Natal	7,198	91	354	256	7,900
Orange Free State	6,685	—	—	—	6,685
Port Elizabeth	1,967	—	—	—	1,967
Potchefstroom	6,415	2	—	4	6,421
Pretoria	14,313	—	—	—	14,313
Rand Afrikaans	2,143	—	—	—	2,143
Rhodes	2,299	—	42	1	2,342
Stellenbosch	9,284	—	—	—	9,284
South Africa	26,981	1,177	2,006	3,995	34,159
The North	—	—	—	1,509	1,509
The Western Cape	—	1,440	—	—	1,440
The Witwatersrand	9,855	28	374	42	10,299
Zululand	—	—	—	1,003	1,003
Totals	95,589	3,142	5,232	7,845	111,808

Source: SA Institute of Race Relations.

THE PRESS AND CENSORSHIP

Following the Prime Minister's warnings to the Press in 1973,[154] the association of newspaper proprietors—The Newspaper Press Union (NPU)—itself proposed strong 'self-disciplinary' measures in an attempt to stave off Government legislation against Press freedom. The main proposal was that the Press Council should be entitled to impose fines of up to R10,000 on newspapers which it finds guilty of 'racial incitement' or other offences. The NPU's move angered journalists, whose representative body, the SA Society of Journalists, had not been consulted. Raymond Louw, editor of the *Rand Daily Mail* (the main target of the Prime Minister's attacks in 1973), rejected the proposed amendments as 'imposing a further form of censorship'. Harry O'Connor, editor of the *Eastern Province Herald.* said: 'If the freedom of the Press is to be curtailed it should be seen to be curtailed by the Government and not by the Press itself.' Joel Mervis, editor-in-chief of the *Sunday Times* said: 'The new proposals are, in my mind, a negation of the basic and established principles of the free Press.' Editors of the pro-Government Afrikaans Press supported the code.

Explaining how the new Press Code would limit Press freedom the *Rand Daily Mail*'s editor pointed out[155] that virtually everything said on race relations 'can have the effect' of stirring up feelings of hostility. A speech by a politician criticizing the political and economic disabilities of blacks 'could have the effect' of stirring up hostility against whites who were regarded as responsible for those disabilities. However, it appeared that the Government's own General Law Amendment Act (see Legal Affairs below), more strongly if ambiguously worded, would be more readily applied than the Press Code. Nevertheless, the Government persisted in its attempts to get the Press to 'discipline itself' rather than be seen to be applying its own curbs. The Minister of Police approached the NPU in October in the hope of obtaining a ban on the reporting of police activity in any 'circumscribed' area of SA. A Bill defined a 'circumscribed area' as any area declared such by the Minister of Justice. It provided that no newspaper, without the Minister's consent, could publish 'any information, detail, rumour or allegation with reference to the numerical strength, presence, actions or activity of members of the police force in a circumscribed area'. Explaining his intentions the Minister of Police[156] said that he was 'not keen' to legislate against the Press and that he had no objection to the reporting of general police activities. He was worried about 'the border situation and the Rhodesian situation', and was trying 'to protect the country from inadvertent help that could be given to its enemies'. The president of the SA Society of Journalists said the legislation as proposed could lead to blanket bans on anything involving the police in any part of the country. He added: 'The Government clearly is adamant to destroy the freedom of the Press in SA. We will resist to the bitter end'. Most English-language newspaper editors firmly resisted the Minister's approaches; some said they would resign sooner than agree.

Considerable publicity was given to the arrest and trial of the editor of the *Natal Daily News*, Michael O'Malley, and another journalist, Michael Green, charged with publishing a report about the planned pro-Frelimo rally in Durban in September. (See Black Politics above.) Both were convicted but appealed.

The Government published a new Publications and Entertainments Bill in 1974. Its most controversial section was the proposed abolition of the existing right of appeal to the Supreme Court against decisions by the Publications Control Board. It set up a Publications Appeal Board whose members were given more protection than afforded by law even to judges and magistrates. *The Star*[157] commented that the new law was 'designed to put censors beyond the law and above the community they are supposed to serve'; it would stifle any public debate on everyday censorship decisions. The Government enacted the Bill despite heavy criticisms.

The Minister of the Interior told Parliament in August that the censors had banned a total of 8,768 publications and 8,728 other 'objects' excluding films since censorship was established in 1963. Only 40 banned publications had subsequently been permitted. During 1973 the Publications Control Board had prohibited 855 publications and 34 'other objects', and 129 full-length feature films; 507 films were approved subject to exhibition only to persons of a particular race or class; 395 were approved subject to excision of a specified portion; only 252 were approved unconditionally. Afrikaans literary circles were disturbed by the banning of *Kennis van die Aand*, by a well-known Afrikaans author, Andre Brink. It was published abroad under the title *Looking on Darkness*. (See Afrikaner Intellectuals above.)

An example of discriminatory handling of the Press occurred in September when the Minister of Justice permitted two Nationalist papers to publish interviews with Neville Curtis, former Nusas president who fled the country (see Students above), but forbade the *Rand Daily Mail* from publishing a similar interview. In protest, the *Mail* appeared with an empty column.

A hint of the nature of SA's television service, when it commences in 1976, was given by the director-general of the SA Broadcasting Corporation, Douglas Fuchs, who said[158] the corporation had 'no intention' of taking a neutral stand over issues of political ideology in its TV programmes. 'Against the attempts of the Western world to impose its pattern on others, the SABC tries to step into the breach for the right of all communities to be themselves and to develop according to their natures. Against the universalists and egalitarians who so irritatingly deal blows against us, we take the view that only the recognition of diversity of peoples promotes the meaningful freedom and harmony for which they strive. In a war of ideas neutrality is no virtue.' One of Fuch's colleagues later made it clear that there would be no TV for blacks[159] 'The enormous cost of TV rules out separate services for the various black groups in the initial stages', said Theo Greyling, SABC's Information and Public Relations officer.

RELIGIOUS AFFAIRS
Despite the SA Government's hostility to the World Council of Churches (WCC) its SA affiliates remained members through the SA Council of Churches. The SACC's

general-secretary, John Rees, attended WCC meetings as well as the All-Africa Conference of Churches (AACC) assembly in Lusaka in May 1974. He unsuccessfully opposed some of the AACC's resolutions condemning SA, white emigration, economic disengagement and support for the liberation armed struggle; but he succeeded in toning down the militancy of some resolutions. Four black South Africans were elected to the AACC executive, one as vice-president.

The SACC continued its own campaign[160] against Government policies. Its national conference in August condemned the Government's plans to move hundreds of thousands of Africans in schemes for Homelands' consolidation. Its most controversial resoltuion was in support of conscientious objection to military service on the ground that it was not a Christian's automatic duty to engage in violence and war whenever the State demanded. While Christians were justified in taking up arms to fight a 'just war', the Republic of SA was at present an unjust and discriminatory society. It was hypocritical to deplore the violence of 'terrorists or freedom fighters', while SA prepared to defend its society 'with its institutionalized violence' by means of yet more violence. The Prime Minister's reaction[161] to the resolution was that the SACC wanted a confrontation with the State. 'I want to warn very seriously that those who play with fire in this way must consider very thoroughly before they burn their fingers irrevocably' (see Defence above).

The SACC's resolution deeply offended the Dutch Reformed Church in SA (NGK). A unanimous motion at the NGK's General Synod in October[162] proclaimed 'the right and duty of every citizen to defend his people and fatherland and to protect the freedom of its citizens'. The Northern Transvaal moderator of the NGK said that SACC resolution had 'slammed the doors' between the two bodies; there was no longer common ground on which to discuss eventual Church unity. The NGK also found itself isolated from its parent church in Holland. The Netherlands Reformed Churches in Europe are members of the WCC and are reported to contribute c. R12,000 a year to the WCC's programme to combat racism (whose funds are distributed between southern African liberation movements). The Reformed Ecumenical Synod in Amsterdam in March agreed with the WCC's policy of discouraging emigration to SA but opposed discouragement of foreign investment. The General Synod of the NGK resolved[163] to regard its ties with the Netherlands Reformed Churches as broken unless the decision to support 'terrorism' on the SA borders was rescinded not later than the first session of the next Synod. An NGK synodical commission produced a 64-page report[164] emphasizing that racial and cultural differences were 'implicity present at the Creation', and that the SA Government's policy of Separate Development had theological 'validity'. However, the NGK's General Synod did accept mixed worship in principle, although with certain reservations. A motion calling on the church to throw open its doors to all worshippers was overwhelmingly rejected, but mixed worship could be permitted if local church councils considered it advisable. An 'emergency committee' of various African independent church associations met to draw up a draft federal constitution aimed at merging some of them. The 'Black Renaissance Convention' was formed in 1974 (see Black Politics above). The formerly banned church leader, Dr Manas Buthelezi, said that the convention had 'reflected a true struggle in which the black community was brought face to face with realities, some of which may be unpleasant. It also gave an impression of self-awareness and solidarity among us.'

SPORT

SA's isolation from world sport increased in 1974 and debate over Government policy produced a serious cleavage in the ruling party. (See Politics above.) The Sports Minister, Dr Koornhof, said that SA was excluded from nine international sporting organizations—weightlifting, swimming, cycling, football, boxing, wrestling, athletics, canoeing and the Olympic Games. During 1973 and the first six months of 1974 South Africans were barred from taking part in 20 sporting events held in other countries, including several which until recently had good sporting relations with SA, e.g. Australia, New Zealand, Argentina, Brazil and Japan. (In June, Japan announced that visas would no longer be granted to South Africans for sporting, cultural or educational reasons.)

The Government's attempt to meet international criticism was to move further in the direction of allowing 'multi-national' but not multi-racial sport. SA sports bodies, under suspension from international bodies, would be permitted to hold 'multi-national' events even when international teams were not present. 'Multi-national' sport allows players of different races to play together in international events but not to play together—even for selection purposes—at home. One concession was to allow mixed sports at club level between local soccer teams of all races provided the games were confined to private club events. In 1975 further concessions were made. (See Politics above.)

LEGAL AFFAIRS
RIOTOUS ASSEMBLIES ACT
The Riotous Assemblies Amendment Act was introduced in February 1974. The Minister of Justice told Parliament that problems had arisen with the principal Act of 1956. The power of magistrates to prohibit gatherings was 'too limited', and the Act sometimes required exact compliance with elaborate formalities 'at a time of emergency'. The Act had also covered only public gatherings in defined public places in the open air. Gatherings in other places could not be prohibited or controlled 'regardless of how dangerous a situation they might create'. The new amendment defines a 'gathering' as meaning any gathering, concourse or procession of any number of persons, whether such purpose be lawful or unlawful. A magistrate can now prohibit any or every gathering at any place or everywhere in his district if he has reason to apprehend that the public peace is seriously threatened. The new amendment also makes it an offence not only to convene, preside at or address a prohibited gathering, but also to attend one

Several gatherings were prohibited under the terms of the new amendment in 1974, including a Sharpeville commemoration in Durban in March; a demonstration against the visit of Paraguay's President in April; demonstrations in Cape Town in August; and all meetings anywhere in the country by Saso and BPC between 24 September and 20 October. Defiance of the latter prohibition led to the mass arrests of late 1974 (see Detentions and Bannings).

GENERAL LAW AMENDMENT ACT
The Second General Law Amendment Act, No. 94 of 1974, was amended to provide that 'any person who utters words, or performs any other act, with intent to cause, encourage or foment feelings of hostility between different population groups of the Republic shall be guilty of an offence and liable, on conviction, to a fine not exceeding R2,000 or to imprisonment for a period not exceeding two years, or to both.' The new legislation was generally interpreted as intended to curb Press freedom.

AFFECTED ORGANIZATIONS ACT
The Affected Organizations Bill was passed which enables the State President to declare any organization 'Affected' if it was deemed that politics were being engaged in, by or through the organization, with the aid or influence of an organization or

person abroad. A registrar of 'Affected' organizations would be appointed with powers to enter premises, examine and seize documents and question persons.

Following the Schlebusch Commission's[165] final report on Nusas, it was the first to be declared 'Affected' (see Students Affairs above). The fifth interim report of Schlebusch said that although the SA Institute of Race Relations (SAIRR) stood for 'change' in SA it could 'by no manner of means be equated with the "change" which other radical organizations or persons have in mind'. The Institute was said to desire 'an evolutionary and peaceful process'. Criticism of the Institute was reserved for its Youth Programme. The Commission recommended that the Government should investigate the Programme 'and then take appropriate steps to eliminate any malpractices. The Commission was also disturbed by evidence that 'within the ranks of the Institute there is a group of radicals, by far the majority of whom are at present, or have been over the past few years, leading lights in Nusas'. These people were stated to be 'out to steer the Institute in a more radical direction for their own purposes, namely as a 'post-university Nusas' and also, if possible, even to take over the Institute'. In a scathing reply to Schlebusch, the SAIRR said that the Government's suggestion that the Government should intervene in the conduct of its Youth Programme was 'gratuitous and unwarranted'.[166] By the end of 1974 the Schlebusch report on the Christian Institute and the University Christian Movement had not been published.

Legal action was taken against those who had refused in 1973 to testify before the Schlebusch Commission.[167] Nine members of Christian Institute and four members of the SAIRR had refused to testify. Dr Beyers Naude of the Christian Institute had his conviction and sentence set aside by the Transvaal Supreme Court, whereupon the cases against others were withdrawn. The passports of several Christian Institute members were subsequently withdrawn.

PASS LAWS

The Deputy Minister of Bantu Administration, Punt Janson, announced that the whole question of pass control regulations was being investigated. Simplification would include dropping the many forms which Africans found difficulty in completing. The police practice of summarily arresting Africans unable to produce their pass books on demand was declared illegal in a decision of the Natal Supreme Court which ruled that Africans ordered to produce their pass books should be given 'reasonable time' to produce them if they were not carrying them at the time. The Minister of Police said that it was not 'practical' for Africans to be allowed reasonable time to fetch their passes. In view of the Court's judgment he was considering introducing even more stringent legislation. Meanwhile, the Government decided to appeal the Court's judgment.

Statistics show a significant decrease in the number of cases sent for trial under the pass laws in recent years.[168] The total number of cases heard in 1971-72 was 615,825; in 1972-73 it had dropped to 515,608, and was likely to have dropped further in 1974 with the abolition of the Masters and Servants Act (see Labour Policy above). The SAIRR pointed out, however, that the 1972-73 figures still amounted to 1,413 trials for pass law offences every day of the year. Articles in the Johannesburg *Star* (3, 4 5 July) described what was termed a system of 'conveyer belt justice' in the Bantu Affairs Commissioners' Courts in Fordsburg, Johannesburg, where each court might deal with between 80 and 130 cases a day.

(For other legal affairs, see The Press, Censorship, Security and Defence, Detentions and Bannings, Student Affairs, Labour Policy and Strikes and Trade Unions.)

POLICE

In 1974 the police force had 19,498 white and 16,031 black members.

Four white and five black policemen were killed in 1973 on the country's borders in security operations, while one white and six black policemen were killed in other actions in the Republic and Namibia. Five white policemen were killed in Rhodesia in March 1974. In the first six months of 1974 the police had shot at and killed 42 blacks, seven Coloureds, and one Asian in the course of their duties.

The deputy head of the Bureau for State Security (BOSS) Brig. M.C.W. Geldenhuys, was appointed head of the Security Police in July in a move interpreted as bringing the Security Police even closer under the wing of BOSS.[169] His predecessor at the Security Police, Lt-Gen. 'Tiny' Venter, was known to have been on bad terms with BOSS and its head, Gen. van den Bergh. The cost of maintaining BOSS was reported to have trebled since its creation in 1969, when R4m was appropriated under the Prime Minister's department. Its operations cost R12.5m in the 1974-75 financial year.[170] The secrecy of BOSS is protected by law and Parliament is forbidden to question its activities. The Prime Minister is directly responsible for BOSS and authorizes its expenditure 'in the national interest'. BOSS is also entitled to refuse to give evidence in any court of law if a Prime Ministerial certificate says that the evidence would be prejudicial to public safety.

PRISONS

Three prison warders were convicted in October and sentenced for assaulting and causing deaths of prisoners. The warders, two white and a black, were jailed for 18 months; two others were given suspended sentences. Mr Justic Hiemstra of the Rand Criminal Court said that the assaults were 'barbaric, cruel and inhuman'; the trial had revealed 'serious evils in the Prisons Department'. He added that there had been evidence of torture and of assaults not being a rare occurrence. As he announced sentence c. 150 black spectators in the public gallery hissed, whistled and shouted: 'They should rot in jail.' Replying to questions in Parliament on 15 October the Minister of Justice said that a letter had been sent to all prison commanding officers strongly condemning assaults and unworthy behaviour in general. The Minister said three prison warders had been killed and 35 seriously injured by prisoners between 1 July 1971 and 30 June 1973. During the same period 36 prisoners had been killed and 113 injured by fellow-prisoners, and 21 killed and 36 injured by warders. Members of the Opposition called for a judicial inquiry into prison conditions, but the Minister said such an inquiry would take at least six years to complete. However, an inquiry was ordered to investigate the penal system in general.

DETENTIONS AND BANNINGS

The Minister of Police told Parliament on 12 February 1974 that he did not think it in the public interest to disclose information about detentions under the Terrorism Act during 1973. He claimed that nobody had died in detention. Later he said that no one had been arrested or detained under the Act during the first six months of 1974. However, in September the police arrested and detained an undisclosed number of people, reported to be members of Saso, the BPC and the Black Allied Workers' Union (Bawu) following the Government's ban on pro-Frelimo rallies. (See Black Politics above.)

In September 19 people were detained (13 in Durban) when the Security Branch carried out raids throughout the Republic on the offices and homes of black leaders. On 30 September 12 more people were arrested. On 15 October, 18 people appeared in court on charges under the Riotous Assemblies Act and remanded awaiting trial. They included two whites—Patricia and Peter Bolton. as well as African and Indian militants—a 17-year-old 'Coloured youth', a 15-year-old 'Indian schoolgirl',

Ndabazoluleka Cele, John Dlamini, Michael Fabre, Kampadassam Govender, Petrus Gumede, Colin Johnson, M. Khanyile, Ronald Matabela, Levelile Moahlola, Mabalengwe Msibi, Cornelius Msomi, Perumal Padayche, Ashlather Rameally and Marian Zeeman. Among those detained and not charged under any Act were Jerry Modisane (banned, former Saso president), J. Nefolovodwe (Saso president) Kaunda Sedibe (SRC president, Turfloop), Nkwe Nkomo (BPC national organizer), Mahlomolo Skosana (BPC assistant organizer), Strini Moodley (banned, Saso official), Dr Aubrey Mokoape (BPC official), Muntu Myeza (Saso secretary-general), Rev. Castro Mayatule (BPC chairman), Lindelwa Mabandla (Bawu), Bridgett Mabandla (SAIRR youth organizer), Cyril Ramaphosa (Saso chairman at Turfloop). At least 15 other Saso and BPC officials were detained. During raids in Cape Town on 7 November the following were detained: Johnny Issel, Steven Carolus, Harold Dixon and Ruben Hare (Saso). Others reported detained include Mandikwe Manthata (ex-vice-chairman of Saso), Drake Koko (banned, BPC and Bawu) and Aubrey Mokoena. The Program for Social Change published a list of six other former Saso leaders.

An application was made before the Supreme Court in November for an order restraining the police from assaulting the detainees.[171] Those named in the order were Lindelwa Mabandla, Saths Cooper, Revabalan Cooper, Mosiouwa Lekotla and Muntu Myeza. The order was refused. Rumours persisted that Kaunda Sedibe (the Turfloop student leader) and two of the Cape Town detainees had died.[172] On 20 November 700 black women delivered a petition to the offices of the Prime Minister and the Minister of Police calling for the release of the detainees. The Program for Social Change listed 19 of those mentioned above as having been charged under Section 6 (1) of the Terrorism Act, which provides for the accused to be held incommunicado indefinitely until the State has completed its investigations.

A large number of other people were still held under various banning orders. The SAIRR survey for 1974 estimated that at the end of April 1974 459 people were still banned. The Minister of Justice said on 9 August that up to the end of June 1974, 72 banning orders were issued; 84 were allowed to expire, two were withdrawn, 11 were renewed, of which four had been renewed once before.

Two black clergymen, Dr Manas Buthelezi and Rev. Hamilton Qambela, had their banning orders removed during 1974. An order in force against Peter Brown, national president of the former Liberal Party, was allowed to lapse in July. Nevertheless, according to legal opinion[173] it remained an offence for anyone to record, publish or disseminate any utterance or writing of Mr Brown's except with the Minister's consent. The banning order on Robert Sobukwe, former PAC leader, was renewed for a further five years in May.

Among those banned for five-year periods during 1974 were three whites who had been involved in the Students' Wages Commission at the University of Natal and in the organization of African trade unions—Halton Cheadle, David Hemson and David Davis—and another trade union activist, Jeanette Murphy. The Minister of Labour said in Parliament that they had been banned for being 'agitators who do not want to make use of the workers' existing constitutional channels, and want to undermine law and order in this country'. The acting Minister of Justice later told a Tucsa delegation that the four had been banned for 'endangering the safety of the State', and not for their trade union activities.

The Prime Minister told an American TV interviewer on 19 April that a banned person was entitled to ask for the reasons why he was banned and 'these reasons are given to him'. On at least two occasions during the year the falsehood of this claim was exposed. Four banned persons wrote to the Minister of Justice asking for the reasons for their banning, only to be informed that 'the information which induced the Minister to issue the notices can, in his opinion, not be disclosed without detriment to public policy'.[174]

Parliament passed a new Act enabling Homeland Authorities to impose certain types of banning orders. The legislative and executive powers of the Republic would, however, be retained in the areas of the Homeland authorities. The Act empowers Homeland authorities to prohibit any organization and its members, or the furtherance of its objects, and to prohibit or restrict any African who is an office-bearer of any such organization; to restrict any African to any area; and to prohibit the publication of any speech, utterance or writing of any African. These powers were subject to the approval of the Minister of Bantu Administration who told Parliament that the Transkei and Ciskei had asked for measures of this nature. Lebowa's Interior Minister, Collins Ramusi, stressed that his Homeland wanted no part of the 'evil powers' of banning.

Apart from removing the passports of leading members of the Christian Institute, including Dr Beyers Naude, a blanket ban was imposed on the entry to SA of all executive members of the World Council of Churches.

POPULATION

Estimates, June 1974: African: 17,745,000, 71.2%; White: 4,160,000, 16.7%; Coloured: 2,306,000, 9.3%; Asian: 709,000, 2.8%; total: 24,920,000. In ten years SA's white population rose by almost 25%, while its African population rose by more than 30%. The white population of 4.16m compares with 3.33m in 1964. The African population of 17.4m compares with 13.49m in 1964. Whites are also outnumbered by two individual black groups: the Zulus and Xhosas, who number 4.63m and 4.76m respectively.

THE GOVERNMENT (reshuffled 1 February 1975)

President-elect	Dr N. Diederichs
Prime Minister	B. J. Vorster
Other Ministers:	
Finance	Senator O. P. F. Horwood
Defence	P. W. Botha
Foreign Affairs	Dr H. Muller
Labour, Posts and Telecommunications	M. Viljoen
Bantu Administration and Development, Bantu Education	M. C. Botha
Transport	S. L. Muller
Information and the Interior	Dr C. P. Mulder
National Education, Social Welfare and Pensions	Senator J. P. van der Spuy
Planning, Environment and Statistics	J. J. Loots
Public Works and Community Development	A. H. du Plessis
Mines, Immigration and Sport	Dr P. G. J. Koornhof
Agriculture	H. Schoeman
Health, Coloured Relations and Rehoboth Affairs	Dr S. W. van der Merwe
Economic Affairs	J. C. Heunis
Tourism and Indian Affairs	Marais Steyn
Justice, Police and Prisons	J. T. Kruger

FOREIGN AFFAIRS

SA's international relations underwent major changes in 1974 mainly as a result of the April coup in Portugal which affected its position both in Africa and the West. The Prime Minister's detente diplomacy, discussed at length in an essay in this volume, produced some early promise of success; but the stumbling block remained Mr Smith in Rhodesia. The Kissinger-Nixon policy of easing US official attitudes to

SA[175] was re-evaluated in Washington. Under a Labour Government, Britain stiffened some of its policies[176] towards Pretoria, mainly on Namibia and by abrogating the Simonstown Agreement. But French policy under President Giscard d'Estaing continued to be fruitful.[177] Japan, under African pressures, began to revise its policies,[178] while Australia and New Zealand continued to toughen their critical stand. SA's greatest success has been in developing its Latin American and Iran relations. The threat of expulsion from membership of the UN had a profoundly disturbing effect on Pretoria.

PORTUGAL, MOZAMBIQUE AND ANGOLA

Following the Portuguese coup d'etat of 25 April 1974, SA gave immediate recognition to the new Government, but in a radio broadcast on 26 April Vorster said the change would affect SA intimately. SA's Foreign Minister later added that SA would have to accept that Portugal's attitude towards SA at the UN would undergo a transformation. This was fully confirmed when Portugal's delegate to the UN, Dr Francisco Ramos da Costa, attacked 'apartheid as practised, apartheid as a policy and apartheid as a principle'. He added: 'We are happy to be able to erase the shame which consisted of seeing the name of Portugal beside those of countries which persist in imposing inhuman and anachronistic racial discrimination through minority hegemony.'

Vorster's attitude to a Frelimo Government in Mozambique was consistent from the beginning: 'A black Government in Mozambique holds no fear for us whatever. We are surrounded by black Governments as it is, and we ourselves are in the process of creating some more by leading our own black Homelands to independence.'[179] Asked if he was worried that a guerrilla organization was taking power he said: 'We are not interested in the personnel of the Government of Mozambique.'[180] Vorster cited events in the Portuguese territories as 'proof' that SA's policy of separate development was right: 'The root of the trouble in all these territories was that the Portuguese policy was one of assimilation—which was a negation of the nationhood of their peoples. The territories were part of metropolitan Portugal, instead of being independent. It just didn't work out.' Vorster's optimism about Frelimo stemmed from his awareness of Mozambique's economic dependence on SA.[181]

After the attempted right-wing *putsch* in Mozambique in September, the SA Government allowed a relief fund to be set up for refugees and allowed 25,000-30,000 to enter the country, but not to stay. However, it maintained its 'correct' position and refused to support the recruitment of white mercenaries for further right-wing attempts. The Foreign Minister told Parliament:[182] 'We do not associate ourselves in any way with colonialism. We hold no brief for it in any shape or form . . . Everyone knows that we are opposed to neo-colonialism.' He added: 'We do not accept that an indigenous Government must necessarily lead to instability and anarchy.' SA's apparently consistent approach was immediately rewarded by a marked toning-down of Frelimo's militancy. The transitional Government leader, Joachim Chissano, told a Press conference in Lourenco Marques[183] that it was 'the duty of the new Government to study the real relations existing between SA and Mozambique and to try to decide on a correct policy'. Frelimo had a policy of non-intervention in the affairs of other countries and did not pretend 'to be Messiahs or saviours of SA'.

In Vorster's now famous detente speech in Nigel on 6 November[184] Vorster was able to speak hopefully about Mozambique honouring past agreements over the ports of Lourenco Marques and Beira, Mozambique labour and the Cabora Bassa power scheme. 'I am glad to be able to tell you that in spite of certain difficulties these agreements will be honoured fairly faithfully,' he announced.

Vorster publicly ignored murmurs of dissatisfaction in his own ranks, such as the

Old Guard spokesman, Ben Schoeman, who said in September that he was afraid of a 'second Congo' in Mozambique and accused the Portuguese Government of having sold the whites in Mozambique to 'the terrorists'. Pro-Government papers like *Die Burger*[185] welcomed such expressions of doubts about what was happening in Mozambique 'because the Government has to talk with restraint and discipline demanded by official international intercourse'. The paper added: 'After all, the truth is that over many years things have been done in Frelimo's name which made civilized people turn pale, and it is not at all certain yet that worse is not to come.'

The Government said in September that its approach to Angola would be the same as to Mozambique, although the situation was more fluid. A complication was the flood of Ovambo refugees into Angola from Namibia.[186] While MPLA and FNLA were reported[187] to be planning guerrilla operations against SA once they gained power the third liberation movement, Unita, said that it wanted only peace with SA and that its policy was non-interference with neighbouring States.

RHODESIA, ZAMBIA AND BLACK AFRICA

(For a full analysis of relations between SA, Rhodesia and Zambia see *Southern Africa: The Secret Diplomacy of Detente* in Part I of this volume.)

The Government's pressure on the Smith regime to reach a settlement with 'his Africans' is reflected in pro-Government newspapers in September 1974. *Die Transvaler* said that SA followed a policy which recognized black national aspirations and ensured them the right of self-determination. 'Fairness, justice, moral responsibility and practicability were the touchstones of SA's race policies.' It added that 'if Rhodesia's race policies run counter to these touchstones, SA would be justified in pointing this out to our neighbours. We cannot and must not identify ourselves with the policy directions of people who do not allow full scope for the freedom and independence of the peoples in Africa—even if they are white and Christian and anti-communist'. *Oggendblad* said that SA expected Rhodesia 'to form a united front with its more moderate black men against the terrorist attacks of the future. If Rhodesia does not do this, a big question mark is placed over Rhodesia's moral right to expect deeper SA involvement in her battle.' In 1974 SA involvement in Rhodesia's security was already reaching considerable proportions with a growing number of military casualties[188] (see Security and Defence above).

Relations with Zambia moved from open hostility in early 1974 to an unprecedented rapprochement at the end of the year. A treason trial opened in Lusaka in February which produced evidence of SA attempts to engineer a coup d'etat in Zambia. It was alleged that 99 Zambians had been recruited in 1972 and 1973 to undergo military training in Namibia for nine months. Three Zambians were sentenced to death in July for their part in the plot.

Relations with Malawi had moved in the opposite direction—from cordiality to coolness after President Banda in April suspended SA recruitment of Malawian miners (see Mines above). Malawi's former dependence on Portuguese-cum-SA support was being replaced by a desire to co-operate with Mozambique's Frelimo Government and more with Zambia.[189] Nevertheless both sides were determined to maintain close relations and there were references from SA to 'fruitful contact and co-operation in many spheres'.

By early 1975 the search for detente had enabled Vorster to visit Liberia for talks with President Tolbert,[190] while the Central African Republic's Finance Minister and some anonymous 'Nigerian businessmen' went to the Republic to discuss trade and aid. SA's rising confidence was such that the Government took space in the British Press to canvass the idea of Johannesburg becoming a potential headquarters for the UN Economic Commission for Africa.[191]

72

LESOTHO, SWAZILAND AND BOTSWANA

Lesotho's assertiveness *vis-à-vis* SA took a new turn at the end of 1974 when its Prime Minister, Chief Jonathan, told a public meeting that his Government was to make a claim to the UN for the 'conquered territory' in the Orange Free State (a reference to land taken by the Boers at the end of the 19th century). He threatened that, if necessary, he would submit a petition to the World Court. He mentioned the sizeable towns of Bethlehem and Winburg as falling within the 'conquered territory'. An initial estimate of the extent of the claim would appear to show that all of the Qwaqwa Homeland would fall within an enlarged Lesotho as well as an isolated part of the Ciskei, although the greater part of the claimed territory is in fact in 'white' SA.

Among several points of tension between Lesotho and SA was the problem of Besotho mine workers in SA,[192] who early in 1974 began returning home at the rate of several thousand a week. (In early 1975 Basotho workers in SA mines were on strike in protest at their own Government's new pay deferment regulations—see Mines above.) Another difference was over the question of political refugees from Lesotho. After the January 1974 disturbances in Lesotho, the Maseru Government claimed that supporters of the opposition Basotho Congress Party (BCP) had fled across the border to SA.[193] Jonathan also said that the rebels had been aided by foreigners—a statement that was taken to refer to SA. Pretoria at first denied that any of the men wanted in connection with the rebellion were in SA, but in February a Lesotho spokesman said his Government had refused an offer to exchange political refugees wanted in SA for men wanted in Lesotho. The deal was 'flatly refused' because Lesotho regarded its 'police station raiders' as criminals and not *bona fide* political refugees.

On 8 April Vorster met Jonathan at Jan Smuts Airport, Johannesburg, to discuss relations. A joint statement said they had 'cleared up certain misunderstandings that had arisen, and reaffirmed their belief and determination that both countries based their relations on the principle of good neighbourliness'. They reiterated the basic principle that neither country would interfere in the domestic affairs of the other; both countries were 'committed to peace in the region and economic progress in the region as a whole.'

Lesotho's total dependence on SA was emphasized in a publication close to the SA Government[194] which claimed that Lesotho took 97% of all her imports from SA, while 53% of her exports went to the Republic. In December 1974 a new monetary agreement was signed between SA, Lesotho and Swaziland after two years' hard bargaining. Gold and foreign exchange transactions would continue as in the past, but provision was made for the issuing of national currencies, which would however be legal tender only within their own countries. Lesotho and Swaziland were assured of access to the SA capital and money markets, while SA would pay compensation which 'shall represent a return on the rand currency circulating in their respective areas'. Botswana withdrew from the talks and announced it would form its own Central Bank and national currency within two years.

The Swaziland Government sent a Ministerial delegation to Pretoria in March 1974, to explore possible co-operation in establishing a thermal power station in Swaziland. In August the Prime Minister, Prince Makhosini Dlamini, said that 'neutrality is the cornerstone of our foreign policy', but added: 'Our policy is self-determination for the people of SA and for majority rule.'

Relations between SA and Botswana were strained by the death on 1 February of Abraham Tiro, a Saso leader who had taken refuge in Botswana.[195] He was killed by a parcel bomb. President Seretse Khama's office condemned the 'inhuman and dastardly manner in which Mr Tiro's life was taken' and pointed out that he had 'incurred the deep displeasure of certain powerful circles in SA'. SA's Minister of Foreign Affairs took 'the strongest exception to the imputations and insinuations of SA involvement in the death of Mr. Tiro' and denied any responsibility for his death.

Later in the year Sir Seretse said there was no future for white minority Governments in Africa and reiterated Botswana's disapproval of SA's racial policies; at the same time he stressed that Botswana had no intention of severing communications with its white neighbours.

WESTERN EUROPE
(Relations with Britain are discussed in *Britain's Year in Africa* in this volume.)

The new French Government of President Giscard d'Estaing appeared to wish only to increase its economic and strategic contacts with SA. It assumed the old role of Britain in sending its navy for manoeuvres with the SA navy. France has made itself far and away the major supplier of arms and military aircraft to SA. The SA air force received in early 1975 its first 16 French Mirage F1 fighter-bombers, an improved version of the Mirage IIIs which the SAAF had been using for some years SA pilots and crews had been for training in France during 1974. A *Radio Johannesburg* commentary (15 November) commended French policies in Africa: 'The secret of France's success has been her concern with the realities of power, political, economic and military, and this characterizes her relationship with SA. Ironically, despite the supply of fighter aircraft and submarines to Pretoria, France maintains better relations with Black Africa than any other of the Western Powers.' The commentator also spoke of co-operation between France, Iran and SA involving 'oil, uranium, mining and nuclear know-how in which respects the resources of the three countries are highly complementary'. The same three countries were 'likewise closely concerned with the defence of the Indian Ocean'.

France's State-run *Electricité de France* announced in June that it was ready to build a nuclear power plant of 1,000 megawatts for SA. Iran had already ordered five similar nuclear plants. French interest in SA uranium followed uncertainties about its formerly safe supplies from Niger, Central African Republic and Gabon.

Dutch concern with SA follows a similar pattern to that in Britain. A group of Dutch employers visited SA in March 1974 to investigate African wages and working conditions. They said afterwards that they opposed the WCC's call for foreign investors to pull out of SA. Their leader, however, was reported to have acknowledged that constraints on trade unionists and workers in SA were 'similar to the experiences of the Dutch when the Germans occupied their country'. They concluded that 'evolution is better than political conflict'. Later in the year there was embarrassment in Dutch Government circles following the news that a large steel company, Estel, was considering setting up a steel industry as part of the Saldanha-Sishen project. Estel has 50% West German participation. The Dutch Government announced assistance for the liberation struggle in Namibia. Twenty-two Dutch political, social, religious and student bodies cabled Vorster in March demanding SA withdrawal from Namibia.

Despite political opposition from West German churches, students and trade unionists, commercial relations between SA and Germany continued to grow. German investments in SA were estimated to be more than R1,000 m in 1974, having grown from R70 m in 1965. Trade between the two countries grew by more than 40% in 1973 alone.[196]

Trade relations with Italy were boosted when an Italian consortium signed a coal contract representing the biggest single foreign investment project ever known in SA. Coal exports to Italy would reach 15 m tons annually by 1983—one of the biggest coal export schemes in the world. The coal would be mined near the Botswana border and pumped through water in pipelines to Richards Bay.

A large Spanish trade mission visited SA in November.

UNITED STATES

Following visits to the US by Dr Connie Mulder and Admiral Hugo Biermann, the SA army commander, during which informal contacts were made at the highest level, it emerged that SA had engaged agents in the US to lobby for a change in American policy on SA.[197] The out-going US Assistant Secretary of State for Africa, David Newsom, said in January 1974 that continuing US-SA contact had helped to bring about change in SA during the previous four years. Newsom's replacement, Donald Easum, reported critically to a Congress sub-committee on a five-week tour of southern Africa at the end of 1974.[198] He described his visit to SA as 'a sobering experience'. Nevertheless, he stressed that the US still condemned SA's approach to race and colour and that these policies inhibited official relationships, but that the US maintained lines of communication 'open to all elements of SA's population'. He said the US had no intention of embarking on any kind of military or naval collaboration with SA. In December 1974 the US cast the only vote against a General Assembly resolution requesting the Security Council to consider action to halt the supply of armaments and military equipment to, and military co-operation with, SA. At the same time the head of the SA Navy was visiting the US for 'private discussion'.[199]

The US decision to abolish its system of sugar quotas and subsidies benefited SA considerably. The additional earnings were estimated at R2 m annually.

THE MIDDLE EAST AND IRAN

Israel's representation in Pretoria became fully ambassadorial in March and Israeli-SA Chambers of Commerce were set up in both countries following a marked increase in trade in 1973. A jointly-owned company, Iskoor, was formed to export SA steel to Israel. After Black Africa's severance of relations with Israel in 1973, Israel ceased to vote consistently against SA at the UN. The former Israeli Defence Minister, Gen. Moshe Dayan, visited SA in September and praised SA troops and military installations, but he expressed criticism of apartheid.

The *Guardian* (Manchester) revealed on 9 September that Jordan had resold a consignment of 41 British-built Centurion tanks and a Tiger-cat missile system to SA. The British Foreign Office confirmed the deal and said the Jordanians had since given assurances that no further transactions of the kind would take place.

The Lebanon broke off formal diplomatic relations with SA in February, but both countries maintained 'Offices of Interest' in each other's capitals. Despite the Arab League's oil embargo on SA ordered in 1973, SA-Arab relations were developed in 1974. After a visit to Saudi Arabia by SA's Ambassador in London, Dr Carel de wet (on a 'private visit'), the Saudi's sent a trade mission to Pretoria early in 1975. Their initial negotiation was over the purchase of gold and prefabricated building machines. Trade was increased with a number of Persian Gulf States.[200]

The Shah of Iran said in Paris[201] that continued friendship with SA was in his country's 'long-term interests' and could not be sacrificed 'to profit the interests of others who sometimes act, shall we say, for emotional reasons'. The President of the Iranian Senate, Senator Shariff Imani, visited SA in May; he said that Iran would never impose oil embargoes on SA while relations between the two countries remained as good as they were. Trade between SA and Iran was worth c. R100m in 1973, and was expected to show substantial increases in 1974, following the signing of a number of new commercial agreements. Iran supplies c. 30% of SA's total oil imports; this is part of a partnership agreement with the parastatal Sasol (see Economy below) in the Natref refinery in which it holds a 17% stake. SA's cement industry won a R3m order for the supply of 200,000 tons of cement, and Iran selected SA's Non-Ferrous Metals to head a consortium to undertake the building and operation of Iran's first copper alloy extrusion plant. The Shah revealed that Iran hoped to extend its 17.5% interest in the Natref refinery, but reports that Iran had taken an even bigger (40%) holding in Sasol were denied by a corporation spokesman in December. A new shipping service between SA and the Persian Gulf was launched in July.

LATIN AMERICA

The Government's only foreign State visitor in 1974 was the President of Paraguay, Alfredo Stroessner. He announced afterwards that the SA Government had given Paraguay a loan of $20m for agricultural development. A further loan was revealed in 1975.

Since 1972, SA has elevated the status of its mission in Brazil from legation to embassy, appointed ambassadors in Uruguay, Paraguay and El Salvador (also accredited to Nicaragua and Costa Rica) and stepped up relations with Panama, Chile, Bolivia and Peru. One result of this rapprochement with Latin America was a comparative absence of hostility to SA in the UN. In the General Assembly voting on whether SA's credentials should be rejected, Costa Rica, Bolivia, Nicaragua and Uruguay voted against rejection, while Paraguay, Brazil, Chile, the Dominican Republic, Guatemala, Honduras, Mexico and Venezuela abstained. Ecuador was absent. In the Security Council vote for SA's expulsion from the UN, Costa Rica was one of the two countries to abstain. Peru, however, voted for expulsion.

There are increasing communciations across the southern Atlantic by SA Airways, Aerolineas Argentinas and Varig (the Brazilian airline), while shipping services were increased in 1974. SA's exports to Latin America have gone well ahead. Brazil took four times the value of SA goods in 1973 (R9m) as in 1969, and Argentina twice as much. Between 1973 and 1974 exports to Bolivia quadrupled and increased sevenfold to Ecuador. Brazil placed valuable orders for uranium and fertilizers in 1974. Government missions visited Brazil, Nicaragua, Paraguay and Uruguay in 1974. Among the profitable development projects in South America involving SA Government and business were a huge hydro-electric scheme between Brazil and Paraguay, an irrigation scheme in Peru, oil exploration in Brazil, and gold, iron-ore and oil exploration in Bolivia.

AUSTRALIA

Australia ended all official trade and investment promotion in SA. The Australian Foreign Affairs Department budget made allowance for contributions to African liberation movements. The Department also announced that it would support any Security Council resolution calling for SA's expulsion from the UN. The Australian cricket tour to SA in 1975 was called off.

New Zealand, under the new Prime Minister, continued to pursue similarly hostile attitudes towards SA.

JAPAN

Japan decided in June to refuse to issue visas to South Africans for sporting, cultural or educational visits. Travellers on business would, however, be exempted from the ruling. The announcement coincided with the opening of the annual conference of Japanese Ambassadors in Africa. The outcome of the conference was that Japan planned to step up its trade and aid in Black Africa while continuing 'normal trade' with SA.[202] Japanese trade with SA passed the $1,000 m mark in 1973 for the first time, with Japanese exports rising 64% to $596 m and SA exports up 31% to $418 m. A Japanese Foreign Ministry official summed up policy as 'continued separation of trade and politics'. Japan stressed that it had no direct investment in SA, but the Japanese Anti-Apartheid Movement alleged that local banks and business houses had extended substantial loans to the SA Government. A London-based Japanese bank said that it would immediately halt loans to SA.[203]

USSR

The first commercial contacts between SA and the Soviet Union were revealed at the end of 1973.[204] An SA pulp and paper producer, Sappi, was involved in installing an oxygen bleaching reactor and a pulp mill in Eastern Siberia.

UNITED NATIONS

On 30 September the UN General Assembly rejected the right of the SA delegation to take its seat in the Assembly by 98 votes to 23, with 14 abstentions. The Foreign Minister, Hilgard Muller, was to have spoken in the Assembly on that day but he withdrew his name. A gesture to appease African opinion was the inclusion in the SA delegation, for the first time, of two non-whites. They were attacked as 'puppets' by Zambia's Foreign Minister. The delegation was, however, permitted to take its seat temporarily while the debate on SA's membership of the UN was in progress. In a major policy speech on 24 October the SA delegate said his Government would do 'everything in our power to move away from discrimination based on race or colour'.[205] An African draft resolution recommending SA's expulsion from the UN because of its racial policies, its refusal to yield Namibia and its violation of the UN boycott of Rhodesia, was defeated in the Security Council on 30 October when France, the UK and the US vetoed it. Ten members voted in favour of the draft and two abstained. On 12 November the General Assembly decided to suspend SA from participating in its current session. The Assembly upheld its President's ruling that, by repeatedly rejecting the credentials of the delegation the Assembly had made clear its refusal to have the SA delegation participate.

The General Assembly on 16 December approved a series of resolutions demanding sanctions against SA for its apartheid policies. The first called on the Security Council to stop the supply of arms and military co-operation with SA; the second called on SA to allow public dissent on apartheid policies and to grant unconditional amnesty to persons imprisoned for their opposition to apartheid; the third authorized the UN committee on apartheid to increase aid to SA liberation movements. The Assembly also condemned foreign economic co-operation with SA and called for SA's exclusion from participation in all international organizations and conferences under UN auspices as long as it continued to practise apartheid.

ECONOMIC AFFAIRS *(R1.62 = £1 sterling)*

The rise in the price of gold—to an average of $165 an ounce in 1974—allowed an acceleration of the growth rate without a marked fall in the foreign reserves. Real GNP rose by 8%, oil imports rose by over $700 m; yet the fall in reserves was only $150 m. Earnings from gold rose from just over $2 billion to over $3½ billion. A contributory factor to the year's success was a bumper agricultural harvest and record world prices for some commodities, notably wheat and sugar—somewhat offset by falls in the price of copper. platinum and wool. The world recession had not yet seriously affected SA in 1974; but prospects for some exports, including fruit (fresh and canned), iron ore and other minerals and metals began to weaken by the end of the year.

Inflation worsened considerably—the official consumer price index rose by 14%. Moreover, because SA's population increases by c. 3% a year, a rapid growth in GNP results in a relatively low rise in *per capita* income. For example, an annual growth rate in GNP of 5%—nearly double that of Britain—produces a rise in income per head of only 1.7%—about half that of Britain. Since the index of food and essential requirements index rose by more than the general consumer price index, the African population was severely affected by inflation, despite the rise in wages. Thus SA needs a high growth rate just to sustain existing rates of employment and income. To stimulate growth the Reserve Bank attempted in late 1973 and early 1974 to keep interest rates low, but this led to a virtual drying up of foreign loans, gold and foreign exchange reserves falling by as much as $100 m a month. The policy was therefore reversed, and interest rates allowed to rise rapidly to 12%. This had the required effect of showing a net inflow on capital account over the year as a whole. However, it also led to a marked slowdown of factory production, rising unemployment and shrinking order books by the end of the year. The SA fiscal and monetary authorities therefore face the dilemma currently familiar elsewhere—how to achieve growth without worsening inflation and the balance of payments or drying up foreign loans. The higher gold price rise of course gives SA a considerable cushion in this respect.[206]

During 1974 there was a steady deterioration in the non-bullion trade account of the balance of payments. The cumulative deficit for the first 11 months of 1974 reached R1,426.4 m—compared with R859.3 m for the whole of 1973. SA's dependence on current high gold prices is illustrated by the fact that $10 an ounce on the average annual price of gold puts 1% onto the GNP—and the reverse is also true.

A major feature of the SA economy today is the increasing emphasis being given to investment by the parastatal organizations. It is hoped that this will cushion SA against world recessionary trends. During 1975, for example, capital investment to the tune of R1,100 m will be spent on the development of electric and nuclear power, iron and steel, the chemical industry, phosphates and fertilizers—all of them wholly or partly owned and financed from Government sources. This enormous total does not include investment in the Railways, the Post Office or the mining industry; nor does it take into account resulting increased expenditure by central or provincial governments. For these same industries the annual capital expenditures are expected to be R1,069 m in 1976; R936 m in 1977; R625 m in 1978 and R 619 m in 1979 —making a grand total of R4,349 m in the coming five years. This figure should be compared with the R2,000 which the Government estimates it will have spent in the five years to 1976 on the whole of the 'physical and human advancement' of all the Bantustans put together. It includes housing in the so-called 'resettlement townships' to which Africans excluded from 'white' areas are sent; all agricultural and industrial development both inside the Bantustans and in the 'border areas', education, health and all other subventions from the SA Government to the Bantustan administrations.[207]

NUCLEAR POWER

By 1974 SA had become one of the three largest uranium producers in the Western world, together with the US and Canada. The Prime Minister announced that SA had 25% of the Western world's uranium reserves; second only to the US, they are estimated at almost a million short tons recoverable on average at c. £15 a lb. By 1980 Western uranium consumption is expected to be over 70,000 tons a year, with output from existing mines expected to supply only 66,000 tons. The demand for uranium is expected to double every five years, ensuring a long-term lucrative market.

SA has also become an important innovator in nuclear technology, and hence a potential member of the world's nuclear club.[208] It has kept its uranium enrichment process a careful secret. This had led to some international scepticism as to the feasibility of the method, said to be the cheapest in the world—30% less than the cheapest foreign operation. Nevertheless, the SA Minister of Mines announced in Parliament in June 1973 that a full-scale prototype plant for the economic enrichment of uranium was to be established at a cost of R550 m. (c.£240 m). The plant would probably be owned by a company registered in SA, with Government participation. A pilot plant, commissioned in 1970, costing R39m and containing about 90% local content began production in 1974.

In August 1973, news leaked out of negotiations between a major fuel-energy concern in West Germany, the Essener Steinkohlen Elektrizitaet Ag (STEAG), and the SA Atomic Energy Board to establish a commission to test the economic feasibility of the new process. In April 1974, a contract was signed between STEAG and the AEB to build a uranium enrichment plant in SA 'to carry out a joint feasibility study of two uranium enrichment processes'. In June, Dr Roux announced that 'further overseas interests are now involved: but he refused to disclose their identities. STEAG (as part of a joint Anglo-Dutch-West German programme) is known to have produced enriched uranium by a version of the centrifuge method known as the 'nozzle process'. It seems virtually certain that this is one of the uranium enrichment processes to be studied in the German-SA venture.

Since the SA authorities have disclosed that their technique is not based on the gas diffusion method—the area in which the French are concentrating—the likeliest possibility is that they are exploring the ion exchange method. This involves the kind of technology used in mineral production, with which South Africans are highly familiar.

About 50% of the uranium to be used in the German-SA venture will come from the Rossing uranium mine in Namibia. Nevertheless, the Bonn Government has approved the deal (or, at any rate, refrained from preventing it), which indicates the high priority they place on the venture. SA is also going ahead with elaborate plans to develop its first nuclear power station—the *Koeberg A*—near Cape Town. This station which will initially have two power sets of 1,000 mw each will use uranium enriched abroad until the local enrichment plant is ready to take over the supply. Each of the two power sets is twice as large as the thermal units, of which there are six, being built at the coal-fired electrical power station at Kriel on the Transvaal highlands. This will be the biggest thermal station in the southern hemisphere. Early in 1974 ESCOM sent out invitations to tender for the Cape plant to nine international consortia representing firms from the US, West Germany, France, Japan and Britain. The South Africans hope that the plant will be in operation by 1982. In March 1974 *The Star* (Johannesburg) reported an American interest in submitting tenders; in April a Tokyo newspaper, *Yomiuri*, announced that Mitsubishi Heavy Industries were negotiating; and in June *The Guardian* (Manchester), among others, announced a possible deal between France and SA in which France would supply nuclear reactors to SA in return for large supplies of uranium.

OIL, COAL, AND COMMUNICATIONS

The measures introduced to conserve oil after the announcement of the Arab boycott continued in operation in 1974. They included limitation on the hours of petrol sales and on traffic speeds, as well as a campaign to encourage new investment in coal-fired installations and conversions from oil-fired ones. But the economy's expansion led to increased oil imports, facilitated by importing a higher proportion of crude oil from Iran, directly or indirectly. There is little sign that the boycott caused more than inconvenience, and the higher gold price enabled SA to cover increased oil prices.

Nevertheless, SA's own search for oil, on and off-shore, was stepped up and is expected to double its investment in 1975. Government's grant to Soekor, the oil exploration corporation, will be increased from R7.5 m to R20 m. Moreover, considerable interest was shown in SA in the fact that Zambian Anglo-American—Zamanglo—invested in oil exploration and refinement through taking a large new interest in Engelhard Minerals and Chemicals (EMC) in a $148 m share deal in June. Zamanglo already had a stake in Trend Exploration, with wells in the US: Canada and Indonesia; but its enlarged holdings in EMC will expand its activities in this field.

Plans for a second oil pipeline from Durban to Johannesburg, to cost R82 m, were announced in 1974. It will run parallel to the existing pipeline for most of the way, but will loop an area of the Eastern Transvaal which is growing rapidly and is now dependent on oil from the Sonarap refinery in Mozambique. The new pipeline, like the old, will be run by the SA Railways and Harbours, which will have to raise c. R600 m in 1975, c. R200 m of which will have to be raised on world capital markets.

Massive injections of overseas capital are also planned for a new coal mining giant called the South Cape Corporation. Under the chairmanship of former Transport Minister, Ben Schoeman, it aims to exploit the rich coal deposits of the northern Transvaal and to launch an export programme. Among the investors are General Mining, the Industrial Development Corporation and Iscor. Italy will be the principal foreign contributor; but capital is also expected from other European countries via Switzerland and Luxembourg. The managing director, Gerald J. Bailey, said that a super-pipeline carrying coal across the Transvaal to Richards Bay, costing R200-R300 m, might prove cheaper than rail transport in the long run.

A French firm, Telspace, will construct SA's first earth satellite station near Pretoria. The contract for two antennae is worth R4m. The first will connect SA's telecommunications with Europe and the US; the second will link it with the East, including Australia and Japan.

RELATIONS WITH THE EEC

SA successfully survived the first application of import duties to her fresh and canned fruit on 1 January 1974 following Britain's joining the EEC—despite considerable previous apprehension about the effects of these duties, together with the effects of much higher freight charges and Britain's falling currency. In the event, the market for SA's fruit was a strong one, partly because inflation in Britain allowed large increases in fruit prices to be absorbed, partly because floods in Australia destroyed a significant proportion of fruit there, and partly because the price of puddings—alternatives to canned fruit—rose even more, because of their sugar content. The volume of fruit sold was therefore marginally up, though proceeds fell from R89m to R84m. In Brussels a Belgian MP's plea that SA and Australian sugar should be considered for special terms of entry to Europe—along with developing Commonwealth cane growers—was rejected. In October, the SA Government clinched negotiations to import c. 300 tons of beef from the EEC 'beef mountain'.

The South and South-East Africa Shipping Conference announced in March that by 1977 it plans to have containerized its service between Europe, SA and south-east Africa.

TRADE

In 1974 the UK was marginally overtaken as SA's chief supplier by West Germany—which in 1973 had ousted the US from second place. Iran, which supplied 30% of SA's crude oil requirements, is now high on the list of SA's suppliers. Exports as a whole rose during the year by 38% to R3.4 billion; while imports were up by 50%

to R4.9 billion. The rise in imports took place mainly in the first part of the year, and consisted largely of machinery and machine tools. The export of Krugerrands rose spectacularly from 0.8 m to over 3.2 m. Diamonds also saw a large increase in price; so that the total value of exports of precious coins and precious and semi-precious stones leapt from R479 m in 1973 to R780 m in 1974. The value of agricultural exports also rose—by 50% to about R1 billion.

INDUSTRY
SA's motor industry stagnated at something like nil growth during 1974. Volkswagen and Leyland both had to be baled out by their parent companies. The infant television industry, by contrast, expanded in a fever of activity in 1974, making ready for the first live television test transmission on 5 May 1975. There will be one channel, broadcasting about five hours a day, half in English and half in Afrikaans; by 1979 there is expected to be another channel, in one or more African languages. The Government has granted import licences for 240,000 semi-knocked-down sets to be assembled in SA to help the new industry. But colour sets are expected to cost c. R1,000, and black and white sets R450. This, together with the licence fees of R36 per annum, will make SA television the most expensive in the world. Manufacture of sets has been limited to six companies, two of them with British links (Rand Barlow which has a royalty agreement with Rediffusion; and Thorn which has a partnership with ITT and some local firms).

Heavy manufacturing industries, such as iron and steel, industrial chemicals and non-ferrous metals show high growth rates and are all expected to enter the export field in 1975. Consumer durables also expanded in 1974, since personal disposable income rose steadily.

MINING
The value of gold mined in 1974 broke all records, rising from R1.77 billion to R2.56 billion, with an average free market price for the year of $156. Output, however, declined—largely because of reductions in grade at some mines, but also because of labour disturbances (see Industrial Affairs above). Costs rose by c. 28% over the industry as a whole to c. $60 an ounce—although this varied from c.$28 an ounce at the very profitable end to c. $155 at the marginal end. The volume output of most other minerals mined in SA rose in 1974; and in the first half of the year zinc and copper in particular showed expanded revenues as well. But by the end of 1974 most base mineral producers were somewhat depressed. Some copper mines have contracted operations; only the large Phalabora operation had made a good profit by the end of 1974. Current output of 220,000 tons a year is expected to rise to over 300,000 by the end of the decade. Platinum had a good year with prices rising from $158 to $190, until the sharp fall in the demand from the motor industry at the end of the year. Antimony, manganese and tin producers all had record years.

Potentially very rich new mineral finds have been made in the north-western Cape—two proven ones by American groups. Phelps Dodge has proved 30m tons of a complex ore-body containing copper, lead, zinc and silver; while Newmont and O'Okiep have a deposit of 94m tons of zinc, with small quantities of lead. Other finds in the area also look promising. According to the Minister of Mines, The metal so far discovered has a value of c. R1 billion.

AGRICULTURE
The volume of production rose by about 24% in 1974. Producers' prices rose by 14% in the first half of the year with increases in all sectors except wool.

81

PARASTATAL CORPORATIONS

SA has an unusually high degree of State control over the commanding heights of the economy. Private enterprise co-exists uneasily with SA's form of State capitalism, operated through the powerful State-controlled 'parastatal' corporations. The 'parastatal empire' dates back to Afrikaner Nationalism's dislike of foreign control in the economy; in the 1920s the Iron and Steel Corporation (Iscor) was set up against the hostile opposition of the mining industry, but it enabled SA to become a major and competitive steelmaker and laid the foundations for the Republic's thriving engineering industry. The financing of the State corporations was achieved from Government funds or by joint ventures with private enterprise through equity participation, loans or debentures. With State backing and partnership, the State schemes injected an impetus into the economy which would not otherwise have occurred.

State control has been systematic and the driving force for economic growth has come through expanding the infrastructure. The Electricity Supply Commission (Escom) has created a network of installed electric capacity, supplying power based on coal at low rates. SA Railways and Harbours (SAR&H) provides road and rail facilities, airports and harbours. The Iron and Steel Corporation (Iscor) provides basic steel and steel products. The SA Coal, Oil and Gas Corporation (Sasol) produces oil from coal and a wide range of chemicals. State participation has also been extended into areas of strategy for national security. The Uranium Corporation (Ucor) exploits SA's uranium reserves (25% of the non-communist world's known reserves) for production and sale as crude concentrate, for research into uranium enrichment and for the development of nuclear power stations. The Armaments Development and Manufacturing Corporation (Armscor) controls all arms and aircraft manufacture, working with foreign companies and domestic industry. The Southern Oil Exploration Corporation (Soekor) initiates and supervises the search for oil—so far unsuccessful. The Industrial Development Corporation (IDC) pursues the creation of manufacturing industry for the viability of the country. The IDC's activities extend from mining and aircraft manufacture to shipping and diverse industries such as textiles, printing and agricultural implements. It also has a share in developing the Rossing uranium deposits in Namibia. State participation has extended into the Homelands through the Bantu Investment Corporation (BIC) and the Xhosa Development Corporation (XDC).

A new example of private and State partnership came with the announcement of Sasol's link-up with African Explosives and Chemicals (AE&CI) in 1974 for one of the biggest industrial schemes in SA to date. AE&CI's principal shareholders are ICI and De Beers. The plan spans ten years and requires investment of R1,000 m, of which R250 m is for the construction of a huge complex at Sasolburg (the base of the oil-from-coal project). R70 m will be spent on companies using the by-products, R132 m for a nitrogen and ammonia plant at Modderfontein, R270 m on expansion of plastics and resins production. These and other chemical establishments illustrate the interlinking of the chemical industry.

Armscor: Since its establishment in 1968 the operations of this corporation have made SA largely self-sufficient in armaments. In 1972, 70% of arms expenditure went to Armscor and its subsidiaries or related private enterprise. All in all, SA produces more than 100 types of ammunition, rifles, sub-machine guns, explosives, cannons, armoured vehicles, electric equipment and aircraft. Among the aircraft made under licence are the Mirage F1 and an Italian-designed short take-off plane. West Germany is also a contributor to the Armscor programme.

Escom: Electricity supplies c. 80% of the country's power. The mining industry is the principal consumer. In 1972 mining took 34.8% of electricity and industry

30.4%. Electricity is cheap in SA in relation to other industrial countries, largely because of the easy avaibility and low production costs of coal. The development of hydro-electric power has been restrained by scarce water resources, but a principal source of hydro-electric power will be the Cabora Bassa scheme in Mozambique, which at full production will provide 8% of power currently generated in the Republic. It is envisaged that by the end of the century installed electrical capacity will be composed of coal-fired power, nuclear power, Swazi coal-fired power, gas turbine power and hydro-electricity. In order to reach its target of increasing its energy supplies more than sevenfold by the year 2000, Escom has projected that capital spending in the 1970s will reach R2,500 m. The role of foreign interests up to 1971 was relatively minor, less than 10%, but there has to be growing dependence on neighbouring countries' power sources—especially in Mozambique, Lesotho, Swaziland, Botswana, Namibia and Angola.

IDC: The Industrial Development Corporation's role since its foundation in 1940 has been one of entrepreneur, manager, financier and consultant. Its total authorization of funds since 1940 has been R1,202 m. It looks for gaps in the manufacturing sector which could be filled by new companies in which it invests jointly with local or foreign interests, or both. The partners contribute capital, management and technical skills. Its main mining ventures are the Phalabora complex and the Rossing uranium mine (both in partnership with Rio Tinto Zinc). It has shipping interests through Safmarine and makes pulp in partnership with Courtaulds. It is scheduled to finance the dry dock development at Richards Bay. IDC created the Phosphate Development Corporation (Foskor) as the basis of a fertilizer industry. It also has the Aluminium Corporation (Alusaf) as a subsidiary. It has established an export credit scheme operated with the Credit Guarantee Insurance Corporation and local banks. The scheme is vital in SA's export drive.

Iscor: The Iron and Steel Corporapion embarked on an unprecedented borrowing programme in 1974, largely for the Sishen-Saldanha scheme. This was however in line with the corporation's main objective: to stimulate the economy without necessarily showing profits. However Iscor was showing a serious loss of R38 m in 1974, compared with profits in preceding years. Private enterprise and the UP Opposition showed concern at Iscor's extensive borrowing, but the Government's aim is clearly to make SA an exporter of steel. At present it provides 80% of the country's needs, but this is already 90% of the entire African continent's production. The Sishen-Saldanha project is designed to put SA into the semi-processed overseas steel market, particularly in Europe. The first iron-ore shipment is planned for 1976, reaching an output of 15 m tons a year by the 1980s. Iscor also plans an ambitious growth in the field of semi-processed minerals such as chrome, vanadium, manganese and asbestos. Its programme depends heavily on foreign investment but this does not contradict the Government's political aims.

Ucor: SA is one of the world's three main sources of supply of uranium, together with the US and Canada. In 1974 it was reported that the US is to provide SA with uranium enrichment for its first nuclear power stations. The Koeberg A station, at Duinefontein, is the first of two Escom planned units of 800 mw 1,000 mw. SA's own uranium enrichment process has reached the stage of a pilot plant, but will not be able to supply sufficient quantities for the first reactors. The Nuclear Fuels Corporation (Nufcor) operates as a non-profit company offering services to the uranium mining companies.

Soekor: Despite a singular lack of success in the search for oil in SA and Namibia, Soekor's operations continue, in partnership with mainly American oil companies.

Sasol: The initial objective of this corporation was to produce oil from coal. The by-products of the industry provided the foundation of a major petrochemical industry. Large quantities of manufactured gas are also produced for the industrial Vaal Triangle. A R40 m expansion programme was launched in 1973 to double the supply of gas. The Sasolburg complex includes one of the world's largest oxygen plants in the world and a nitrogenous fertilizer plant. A synthetic rubber plant has also been established and plastic is another off-shoot of Sasol products. A second oil-from-coal plant costing c. R1,050 m was announced at the end of 1974, with a capacity ten times that of Sasol I. It will be built in the eastern Transvaal. Funds will be raised by the State from taxpayers and part of the balance from the Strategic Oil Fund. Sasol already supplies c. 8% of SA's petrol. Ultimately the annual output of petrol from Sasol II will reach 17 m tons—28% of projected demand in the 1980s.

The National Iran Oil Company holds a 17½% interest in the Natref oil refinery, which is an R80 m Sasol venture which began operations in 1971. Its capacity is 2.5 m tons of crude per year. Sasol has a 52½% share in Natref and Total (French) 30%. Another Sasol project with international involvement is a R25 m chemical plant—a joint venture between Sentrachem and Farbwerke Hoechst AS (Germany) for the production of high density polyethylene.

SCHEDULE OF ESTIMATED EXPENDITURE ON SOME MAJOR CAPITAL PROJECTS (million Rand)

	1975	1976	1977	1978	1979
1. Escom	265	265	265	NA	NA
2. Iscor—main works	324	324	324	324	324
—Sishen-Saldanha	116	58	—	—	—
3. Sasol	150	150	150	150	150
4. AE & CI	100	100	100	100	100

Source: Standard Bank.

BUDGET

Dr Diederichs presented his budget in August. Its main provisions were:[209] Sales duty: Current 10%-15% duty on household articles reduced to 5%. Reductions of 5% on a variety of other goods, including watches, musical instruments, toys and sporting equipment.

Stamp and transfer duties: All transfer and stamp duties on fixed property to be consolidated into a single transfer duty payable by the purchaser. Transfer duty for companies to be a uniform 5%—previously company property changed ownership by means of a transfer of shares at 1% stamp duty. Transfer duty for individuals reduced from 3% on the first R10,000, and 4% on the balance, to 1% on the first R20,000 and 3% above that. Stamp duty abolished on affidavits, arbitrations and awards, bills of lading, brokers' notes, etc. Stamp duty on mortgage bonds to be a uniform 20c per R100 instead of the present sliding scale. Bond registration fee of R2,50 abolished.

Personal tax: Surcharge of 10% on personal tax reduced to 5%, thereby reducing maximum marginal tax rate from 66% to 63%. Primary abatements increased by R200 and R100 for married and unmarried taxpayers to R1,200 and R700 respectively. Abatements for children up from R450 to R500 for each of first two children, and from R550 to R600 for each additional child. Also an extra abatement of R200 in the year of birth. The abatement for medical expenditure, insurance premiums, provident and medical aid fund contributions up from R600 and R500 to R700 and R600 for married and unmarried persons respectively.

Married women: Tax deductible allowance of R500 in respect of married woman's earnings raised to R600.

Pensions: Civil pensions increased by 10% from 1 October. White social pensioners to receive an extra R5 per month. Similar increases for social and civil non-white pensions will narrow the gap between race groups. Allowances to foster parents and children's homes raised.

Training: Grants to industrialists from an industry training fund to be fully deductible from taxable income (previously one half was deductible). Employers' expenditure on approved training schemes for African labour to qualify for a 200% deduction in white areas and a 225% deduction in economic development areas.

Investment and initial allowances: Investment allowances on factory buildings unchanged. On machinery, present allowance of 20% (55% in economic development areas) is increased to 25% (60%). Initial allowance of 15% (30% in economic development areas) raised to 25% (40%).

Export incentives: An extra R17 m for the IDC for low interest loans to industrialists establishing export capacity.

Finance charges: Maximum charge for money loans raised from 12% to 14% for all loans exceeding R400. Other finance charges remain unchanged.

Foreign loans: Private sector authorized to seek loans abroad with a duration of six months (previously one year) or longer for approved purposes. Forward exchange cover extended to imports of capital goods requiring extended credit.

Public service bursaries: Bursaries for full-time university students up from R800 to R1,000. Part-timers to get R300—R50 more than at present. Full-time technical college students' bursaries also increased.

Housing subsidy: Maximum value of a house qualifying for a subsidy on bond interest up from R18,000 to R20,000. But the bond ceiling remains at R15,000.

Mining Tax: Gold mines' allowances on unredeemed capital expenditure increased from 8% to 10% for mines granted a mining lease in the future. Non-gold mines to be permitted to write-off unredeemed balance of capital expenditure over a maximum of five years, previously 30 years. Maximum write-off period for gold mines remains at four years.

Company tax: Loan levy on companies halved from 10% to 5% of tax for diamond mining companies and from 5% to 2,5% for others.

Commenting on the Budget, the *Financial Mail* (Johannesburg)[210] wrote on 23 August 1974: Last week we condemned the Budget on the grounds of equity. Our assessment was a gut reaction on Wednesday night. Maturer reflection suggests the Budget is not unjust; it is iniquitous. It heavily taxes the poor through inflation, yet offers, for instance, improved tax-free investments that are of use only to the rich. It provides for hundreds of millions more on defence, but contributes comparatively so little more in absolute terms for African education that hundreds of thousands of children must still go without classrooms or teachers. It reduces by half the tax surcharge paid only by relatively well-off households, yet provides nothing for wider or more generous food subsidy formulae for the very poor.

Transfer duty reductions will make it cheaper for those who can afford to buy their own homes; for those who cannot afford them and may not even buy land to use as surety, Pretoria's housing programme is hopelessly inadequate and thousands must remain homeless. And with the State coffers so full, why no extension of unemployment relief to embrace those hundreds of thousands of African workers earning less than R10,50 a week? With Government spending none the less bounding ahead by a quarter, pressure on scarce resources—skilled labour, capital, foreign exchange— must mount. So inflation will get worse, causing growing hardship in the townships and reserves and driving thousands more children towards malnutrition and starvation. That, in a country that can boast the highest per capita GNP in Africa (apart from oil-rich Libya) is iniquitous in any man's language.

Old-age pensions for whites have been raised by a margin (9.6%) that is lower than the historic inflation rate. While pensions for others have been increased by a greater percentage—for instance, those for Africans by 21,6%—the actual cash increase is pitifully inadequate. Africans will get only $2 per month more. What is that worth at current rates of inflation?

Another issue that could do with a second look is the overall level of government spending. Who says it cannot be cut? The *FM* has taken a look at the Estimates of State Expenditure for 1974-75. It is not difficult to pick out items that look eminently trimmable: About 12% of Government expenditure goes on salaries and wages. Could not the Weather Bureau, for example, dispense with some of its 279 employees (salaries: over R1 m) and the Department of Immigration with some of its officers abroad? The salary bill for those in the UK, for example, amounts to nearly alone; Did you know that the Department of Bantu Administration and Development expects to spend more than six times as much on telephone calls (R307,000) as on the promotion of African sport and recreation? And it is disconcerting to learn that the 90 officials at the Department of Sport and Recreation will be spending an average of R246 each this year on telephone calls alone—that is about 25 local calls each every day! There seems to be some room for heavy cuts in motor transport services. The mind boggles at the estimate that Water Affairs officials will use GG cars to cover a distance equivalent to 1,000 trips round the world. SA's representative at the IMF in Washington is to get a new residence costing R400,000 while the new Chancery and residence for our Ambassador in Bonn will cost R4,4 m, of which R2 m will be spent this year.

ECONOMIC INDICATORS (Seasonally adjusted)

	Month	adjusted figure	One month	One year*
			Percentage change	
Prices				
Consumer—all items (1970=100)	August 1974	141.5	+ 1.7	+13.2
Food (1970=100)	August 1974	156.4	+ 2.4	+19.0
Services (1970=100)	July 1974	138.1	+ 1.0	+ 7.8
Wholesale—all items (1970=100)	July 1974	154.8	+ 1.6	+19.4
External Trade				
Imports (R million)†	August 1974	411.3	- 9.7	+42.6
Exports (R million)†	August 1974	305.8	+24.4	+55.4
Gold and foreign exchange reserves	August 1974	729.0	- 7.1	+21.3
Commerce				
New car sales (number)	August 1974	18,407	- 5.4	-10.2
Commercial vehicle sales (number)	August 1974	9,125	-14.6	- 3.2
Retail sales (1960/61=100)	July 1974	355.4	+ 3.2	+24.5
Wholesale sales (1960/61=100)	June 1974	351.1	- 0.3	+36.9
Manufacturing				
Physical volume of production (1963/64=100)	July 1974	198.6	+ 3.8	+ 9.3
Unfilled orders (R million)	May 1974	1,095.6	+ 3.8	+33.6
Construction				
Building plans passed (R million)	July 1974	94.5	- 4.4	+ 2.8
Buildings completed (R million)	July 1974	67.1	+10.2	+21.0
Cement production ('000 metric tons)	July 1974	643	+ 5.1	+11.7
Other Indicators				
Unemployment (number)	June 1974	7,972	- 2.5	-24.1
Bank debits (1968=100)	July 1974	288.5	+11.6	+32.0
Railway tons/kilometres (million)	July 1974	5,864	+13.5	+14.5
Companies liquidated (number)*	April 1974	63	-16.0	+ 8.6

* Not seasonally adjusted.
† Excluding oil.

SOUTH AFRICA'S FOREIGN TRADE (R million)

Selected Exports	Jan–Aug 1973	1974	Percentage change
Precious and semi-precious stones	332.2	479.5	+44.3
Base metals	233.0	300.3	+28.9
Prepared foodstuffs	191.6	280.0	+46.1
Vegetable products	184.3	219.1	+18.9
Mineral products*	139.1	175.5	+26.2
Textiles and textile articles	130.4	113.3	-13.1
Chemical and allied products	57.9	80.6	+39.2
Machinery and appliances	67.8	78.8	+17.7
Other	294.9	377.0	+27.8
	1,631.2	2,104.1	+29.0
Selected Imports			
Machinery and appliances	629.2	822.8	+30.8
Vehicles and transport equipment	398.6	499.9	+25.4
Textiles and textile articles	202.4	337.8	+66.9
Base metals	144.5	296.4	+105.1
Chemical and allied products	164.5	267.5	+62.6
Paper and paper products	75.8	118.9	+56.9
Optical and photographic instruments	82.2	115.7	+41.1
Mineral products*	26.7	60.7	+127.3
Other	363.9	591.7	+62.6
	2,087.8	3,111.4	+49.0

* Excluding oil.

Source: Standard Bank.

TOTAL ANNUAL TRADE (R million)—axcluding oil and gold.
(including Botswana, Lesotho, Namibia and Swaziland)

	1973	1974*
Exports	2,421.3	3,352.6
Imports	3,275.4	4,914.0
Balance	-854.1	-1,561.4

* Provisional figures.

Source: Barclays Bank.

NOTES

(All the references are to South African publications unless otherwise stated.)

1. See *Africa Contemporary Record (ACR)* 1968-69, pp. 286-346; *ACR* 1969-70, p. B271-310; *ACR* 1970-71, p. B489-532; *ACR* 1972-73, p. B360-414; *ACR* 1973-74, p. B400-473. Also see *Africa Contemporary Record* Current Affairs Series: *SA 1972: A Year of Great Decision; A Republic in Trouble*: SA 1972-73; *Afrikaner Politics in Trouble*, 1973.
2. See essay on *Portugal's Year in Africa* in this volume.
3. See essay on *Southern Africa: The Secret Diplomacy of Detente* in this volume.
4. Interview with Adam Payne in the *Rand Daily Mail*, 9 December 1974.
5. *Rand Daily Mail*, 16 December 1974.
6. *The Star*, 19 October 1974.
7. For earlier warnings see *ACR* 1973-74, p. B 402; *ACR* 1972-73, p. B 362; *ACR* 1971-72, p. B 342.
8. Quoted in the *Rand Daily Mail*, 7 November 1974.
9. *The Star*, 4 January 1975.
10. *The Star*, 21 December 1974.
11. *Ibid*.
12. *Ibid*, 21 October 1974.
13. *Sunday Times*, 8 December 1974.

14. *Rand Daily Mail*, 4 October 1974.
15. *Rand Daily Mail*, 10 August 1974.
16. *Sunday Times*, 15 September 1974.
17. *Rand Daily Mail*, 14 November 1974.
18. *Ibid*, 11 June 1974.
19. *The Star*, 30 November 1974.
20. *Rand Daily Mail*, 30 October 1974.
21. *Ibid*, 31 July 1974.
22. *The Guardian*, Manchester, 24 January 1975.
23. *Rand Daily Mail*, 13 December 1974.
24. See *ACR* 1970-71, p. B 491.
25. See *ACR* 1973-74, p. B 405.
26. *Rand Daily Mail*, 18 November 1974.
27. *Ibid*, 23 March 1974.
28. *Ibid*, 16 March 1974.
29. *Sunday Times*, 3 March 1974.
30. *Ibid*, 22 September 1974.
31. *Ibid*, 3 March 1974.
32. *Rand Daily Mail*, 10 October 1974.
33. See *ACR* 1973-74, p. B 400.
34. *Quoted in the Sunday Times*, 29 September 1974.
35. *Sunday Times*, 15 September 1974.
36. See *ACR* 1969-70, p. B 272.
37. *Sunday Times*, 15 September 1974.
38. *Ibid*, 1 November 1974.
39. *Rand Daily Mail*, 3 December 1974.
40. *The Star*, 6 July 1974.
41. See *ACR* 1973-74, pp. B 408, 413; *ACR* 1972-73, p. B 363; *ACR* 1971-72, p. B 325; *ACR* 1970-71, p. B 489; *ACR* 1969-70, p. B 274.
42. See *ACR* 1973-74, pp. B 408, 434, 454, 617; *ACR* 1972-73, p. B 363.
43. Quoted in the *Sunday Times*, 25 August 1974.
44. J. H. P. Serfontein, *Sunday Times*, 1 September 1974.
45. *Die Transvaler*, 13 September 1974.
46. *Rapport*, 8 September 1974.
47, See *ACR* 1973-74, p. B 402-410; *ACR* 1972-73, p. B 362.
48. See *ACR* 1973-74, p. B 410.
49. For previous references to the Afrikaner Mood see *ACR* 1973-74, p. B 410; *ACR* 1972-73, p. B 366; *ACR* 1971-72, p. B 328.
50. *Rand Daily Mail*, 17 December 1974.
51. *The Star*, 7 December 1974.
52. *Sunday Times*, 17 November 1974.
53. *The Star*, 10 August 1974.
54. *Ibid*.
55. *Rand Daily Mail*, 17 December 1974.
56. *The Afrikaners: Youth and Change*: Optima, Johannesburg, Vol 24 No 2, 1974.
57. H. van de Spuy: *The Psychology of SA—New Society*, London, 12 December 1974.
58. *Rand Daily Mail*, 10 May 1974.
59. Quoted in *The Star*, 12 October 1974.
60. *Rand Daily Mail*, 10 October 1974.
61. *Ibid*
62. *ACR* 1973-74, p. B 449-450.
63. See *ACR* 1973-74, p. B 413.
64. *Sunday Times*, 6 October 1974.
65. See *ACR* 1973-74, p. B 411; *ACR* 1972-73, p. B 366.
66. J. H. P. Serfonken in the *Sunday Times*, 8 September 1974.
67. *Ibid*, 6 October 1974.
68. *Die Vaderland*, quoted in *Sunday Times*, 13 October 1974.
69. *Rand Daily Mail*, 7 October 1974.
70. *Ibid*, 26 March 1974.
71. *Ibid*, 9 July 1974.
72. See *ACR* 1973-74, p. B 417.
73. *Rand Daily Mail*, 19 October 1974.
74. See *ACR* 1973-74, p. B 414; *ACR* 1972-73, p. B 367; *ACR* 1971-72, p. B 481; *ACR* 1970-71, p. B 324; *ACR* 1969-70, p. 272.
75. See *ACR* 1973-74, p. B 417.

76. See *ACR* 1973-74, p. B 369.
77. *Rand Daily Mail*, 19 October 1974. In his report Patrick Laurence provides an interesting background to developments at Turfloop.
78. See *ACR* 1973-74, p. B 416.
79. See *ACR* 1973-74, p. B 417.
80. See *ACR* 1973-74, p. B 415.
81. Also see *ACR* 1973-74, p. B 431.
82. *Rand Daily Mail*, 23 October 1974.
83. Also see *ACR* 1973-74, p. B 425.
84. *Ibid*.
85. See *A Place Called Dimbaza*, African Publications Trust, London, 1974. Also see *ACR* 1973-74, p. B 452.
86. Also see *ACR* 1973-74, p. B 426.
87. *Ibid*.
88. *Ibid*, p. B 427.
89. *Ibid*, p. B 421.
90. *Ibid*, p. B 428.
91. *Ibid*.
92. *Ibid*, p. 329.
93. *Ibid*.
94. *The Star*, 23 March 1974.
95. See *ACR* 1973-74, p. B 429.
96. *Ibid*, p. B 431.
97. *Rand Daily Mail*, 25 July 1974.
98. Summarized in the *Rand Daily Mail*, 30 November 1974.
99. *The Star*, 26 October 1974.
100. *Rand Daily Mail*, 7 September 1974.
101. See *ACR* 1969-70, p. B 281.
102. *The Star*, 11 September 1974.
103. *Ibid*, 24 July 1974.
104. *Rand Daily Mail*, 20 August 1974.
105. *Ibid*, 20 and 23 August 1974.
106. See *ACR* 1973-74, p. B 434.
107. *Ibid*, p. B 447.
108. Summarized in *A Survey of Race Relations in SA* 74, SAIRR, Johannesburg.
109. *Rand Daily Mail*, 14 September 1974.
110. *The Star*, 17 August 1974.
111. *Ibid*, 14 and 15 June 1974.
112. *Rand Daily Mail*, 3 August 1974.
113. *The Star*, 14 December 1974.
114. *Ibid*, 10 August 1974.
115. *Rand Daily Mail*, 10 August 1974.
116. *Financial Mail*, 8 November 1974.
117. See essay on *Britain's Year in Africa* in this volume.
118. *The Star*, 14 December 1974.
119. *Rand Daily Mail*, 16 December 1974.
120. See Francis Wilson.
121. See *ACR* 1973-74, p. B 440.
122. *The Star*, 6 July 1974.
123. *Financial Times*, London, 14 August 1974.
124. *Rand Daily Mail*, 30 November 1974.
125. *Ibid*, 13 June 1974.
126. See *ACR* 1973-74, p. B 438.
127. Stanley Uys in *The Observer Foreign News Service*, 17 September 1974.
128. See *ACR* 1973-74, p. B 444.
129. *Sunday Times*, 27 January 1974.
130. *Ibid*.
131. *Observer Foreign News Service*, 17 September 1974.
132. *Financial Mail*, 18 October 1974.
133. *Rand Daily Mail*, 19 September 1974.
134. *Ibid*, 15 November 1974.
135. *Ibid*, 30 September 1974.
136. *Ibid*, 25 July 1974.
137. *Ibid*, 18 July 1974.
138. *Financial Mail*, 26 July 1974.

139.   *Rand Daily Mail*, 7 November 1974.
140.   See *ACR* 1973-74, p. B 443.
141.   Also see essay on *Britain's Year in Africa* in this volume.
142.   *Rand Daily Mail*, 23 November 1974.
143.   *Ibid*, 25 November 1974.
144.   *Sunday Times*, 13 January 1974.
145.   Quoted in *The Star*, 6 July 1974.
146.   Also see *ACR* 1973-74, p. B 451.
147.   *Africa Publications Trust*, London, 1974.
148.   *Rand Daily Mail*, 5 July 1974.
149.   *Ibid*, 23 July 1974.
150.   *Ibid*, 2 August 1974.
151.   20 October 1974. *Ibid*.
152.   *Ibid*, 16 October 1974.
153.   For further details see XRay on Southern Africa, Fact Sheet, Vol 3, No 9, and Vol 3 No 10, 1974; Africa Brueau, London.
154.   See *ACR* 1973-74, p. B 454.
155.   *Rand Daily Mail*, 11 August 1974.
156.   *Ibid*, 19 October 1974.
157.   *The Star*, 7 September 1974.
158.   *Ibid*, 13 July 1974.
159.   *Sunday Times*, 4 August 1974.
160.   See *ACR* 1973-74, p. B 453.
161.   *The Star*, 3 August 1974.
162.   *Ibid*, 26 October 1974.
163.   *Rand Daily Mail*, 17 October 1974.
164.   *The Star*, 26 October 1974.
165.   See *ACR* 1973-74, p. B 477.
166.   See SAIRR *op cit*.
167.   See *ACR* 1973-74, p. B 448.
168.   SAIRR, *op cit*.
169.   *Sunday Times*, 7 July 1974.
170.   *Ibid*, 25 August 1974.
171.   For details of the allegations see *Rand Daily Mail*, 8 November 1974.
172.   *Sunday Times*, 10 November 1974.
173.   *Rand Daily Mail*, 1 August 1974.
174.   SAIRR, *op cit*.
175.   See essay on *US Year in Africa* in this volume.
176.   See essay on *Britain's Year in Africa* in this volume.
177.   See essay on *France's Year in Africa* in this volume.
178.   See essay on *Japan's Year in Africa* in this volume.
179.   *Newsweek*, Washington, 16 September 1974.
180.   For other details of Vorster's attitude to Frelimo see essay on *Southern Africa: The Secret Diplomacy of Detente* in this volume.
181.   *Ibid*. Also see chapter on Mozambique.
182.   *Rand Daily Mail*, 11 September 1974.
183.   *The Star*, 17 September 1974.
184.   See essay on *Southern Africa: The Secret Diplomacy of Detente*, *op cit*.
185.   *Die Burger*, 16 September 1974.
186.   See chapter on Namibia.
187.   *Sunday Times*, 17 November 1974.
188.   See chapter on Rhodesia.
189.   See chapter on Malawi.
190.   See chapter on Liberia.
191.   *The Guardian*, Manchester, 28 February 1975.
192.   See *ACR* 1973-74, p. B 458.
193.   See chapter on Lesotho.
194.   R. Bodenmüller: *Botswana, Lesotho and Swaziland: their external relations, policy and attitude towards SA*, Africa Institute, Pretoria, 1973.
195.   See *ACR* 1973-74, pp. B 369 and B 436.
196.   See essay on *West Germany's Year in Africa* in this volume.
197.   See essay on *US Policy in Africa* in this volume.
198.   *Rand Daily Mail*, 28 November 1974.
199.   *Sunday Times*, 3 November 1974.
200.   *Sunday Express*, 2 June 1974; *Sunday Times*, 30 June 1974; *Financial Mail*.

201. *Jeune Afrique*, Paris, 11 April 1974.
202. See essay on *Japan's Year in Africa* in this volume.
203. *The Star*, 11 September 1974.
204. *Rand Daily Mail*, 9 November 1973.
205. See essay on *Southern Africa: The Secret Diplomacy of Detente* in this volume.
206. *Financial Times*, Survey of South Africa, London 25 February 1975.
207. Dr A. J. A. Roux, chairman of SA National Institute for Metallurgy, *Rhodesia Herald*, 19 December 1974.
208. *XRay on Southern Africa*, Fact Sheet No 39, Vol 4, No 12, Africa Bureau, London.
209. *Financial Mail*, 16 August 1974.
210. *Ibid*.